"How refreshing it is to have someone acknowledge things for how they really are. Oftentimes we are more comfortable with embracing lies than facing painful truths concerning relationships. Counterfeit love has become normal because our sisters have lost a sense of hope that true love exists. What's profound about your approach is that you bring to light that true love comes at a high price. It's much more than personal pleasure and emotional comfort...which the 'counterfeit' promises. True love is eternal in nature and never fails...it can withstand the most intense heat. True love is not driven to 'get' but to 'give.' True love will stand the test of time.

Because of your forthrightness and courage to address this issue of counterfeit love, many women will be liberated. May God's grace be multiplied to you in this next phase of your ministry as you continue to stand fast in the liberty where Christ has made you free! I am proud to be your brother."
—Gerard Henry, host of the BET gospel show *Lift Every Voice*

"With an ever growing need in us to be loved, it is important to know what is and what is not love. This book identifies the lies and the truth about love. Get ready to go through spiritual rehab as Elder Vikki Johnson reveals the addictions to what is NOT and leads you through your lifelong deliverance to what IS real love."
—Lisa McClendon, gospel recording artist, Diamond Girl Music

Vikki Johnson

Addicted to COUNTERFEIT LOVE

ADDICTED TO COUNTERFEIT LOVE

A New Spirit Novel

ISBN-13: 978-0-373-83038-1
ISBN-10:   0-373-83038-6

www.kimanipress.com

Printed in U.S.A.

This book is dedicated to my daughter, the greatest gift of love given to me. You inspire me to stay whole!

It is also dedicated to the women who will read this book and realize that they deserve to be embraced by real love.

Acknowledgment

I want to thank my Lord and Savior Jesus Christ for surrounding me with your favor as a shield and for keeping ALL of YOUR promises to me. You did it again.

I honor my parents, Joyce Kennedy, Art and Daisy Kennedy for their continued love and support of all that I am and all that I am becoming. I have the best siblings, nieces, nephews and godchildren in the world. I LOVE EACH OF YOU. Everything I do is for us!

Bryce Khambrel—I think of you every single day...your best days are ahead of you!!!

To Linda Gill, Glenda Howard and the entire Harlequin/Kimani family—thank you for empowering my pen to impact the world.

God knew just what I needed and sent me to Kingdom Worship Center in Towson, Maryland. I love you, Bishop Ralph and Deborah Dennis—more than you will ever know.

Again, I'm thankful for my partners in ministry and business: BET, VGR/JEG, Heaven 1580 AM, KWC Women's Ministry, Elder Vikki Johnson Ministries Team, VM Direct and Warm Spirit, who constantly show me nothing but "real love."

To Carol Foster, "Mama" Arla Scott, Marsina Jackson and the staff of DCYE—thank you for sowing seeds in my daughter's life that will produce fruit for years to come. Your vision, love and commitment is a gift to the arts.

Friendship is a gift that I will always treasure. I have a wonderful, talented, anointed "circle of love" in my life who somehow know just what I need to hear and when; who know just what to do and how; who know how to cover me and why. This list is *NOT* all-inclusive, but I must mention the following people because...that's between me and each of them:

Betty Nelson, Kathy Queen, Veda & Marvin McCoy, Vivian Smallwood, Portia & Gordon Wheatley, Aleathea & David Dupree, Juliet Gay, Kellie Carroll, Pam & Mike Pugh, Sher'ri Williams, Mykel Trahan, Latonia Muhammad, Tia Langdon, Marie Taylor, Kym "Outerskinz" Lee, Marie Mouzone, Jennifer "Undercover" Raiford, Crystal Shaw, Sonya Lockett, Kelli Lawson; Roz Holmes, Carma "Baby Jigga" Hammuck, Lyntina Townsend, Gerald Scott, Russell & Susan Webster, Wayne & Barbara Waller; Israel Bell, Darien & Daffney Dennis, Derek Triplett, Carmen Calhoun, Lisa Kemp Williams, Sonya Pass, Lisa McClendon, Jazzy Jordan, Gessie Thompson, Cheryl Jackson, John Deadwyler, Lois & Kevin James, AJ & Charlotte Wright, Dominique "still standing" Watson, Denise "Spare Hands" Brown, Jacquie & Kevin Carter, Annette Anderson, Reggie & Tracy Hopkins, Andrew Carr, Lynette Young, Dr. Kecia DeCosta, Gerard & Terry Henry, LaJoyce Brookshire, Felicia & Mike Stewart and most recently, Apostle Louis & Karen Greenup.

A note to the Reader...

A lie is the *intent to deceive.* Everything that the devil says, does or presents is a lie. He is, by nature, devoid of love and truth. He is the father of lies, so lies are the only kinds of seed he can plant in the wombs of our minds. His intent is *always* to deceive. Even when what he says, does or presents comes wrapped in something that looks true, sounds true or feels true, the intent is *always* to deceive. Consequently, anything the devil says, gives or does has no value: it's counterfeit. It may look real, feel real, sound real, but it is not real.

Love and truth give value. God is love and His word is truth. Everything God says (or doesn't say), does (or doesn't do), gives (or doesn't give) is in, for and through love and truth. This is the foundational reality of our being able to trust Him. Why is this important? It is important because if you don't trust the value of His love and truth in and for your life, you will accept what is not of value: a counterfeit. When the counterfeit relationship doesn't work out (and it won't), you'll think you've lost something of value when in reality, all you've lost is a lie... a counterfeit. Understanding this could save you a lot of time crying, grieving and/or being angry over something that values nothing.

God does not want you to accept the counterfeit. The question then becomes, how can you recognize the counterfeit? You recognize counterfeit relationships—potential or realized—the same way you recognize counterfeit paper money from real paper money. First, you familiarize yourself with the real thing. Second, you hold what could be counterfeit up to the light so you can *check* for the real thing. If you're not familiar with the real thing, when the counterfeit comes, you'll fall for it every time. Even when you *are* familiar with the real thing, if you don't hold it up to the light, you can still be fooled.

God's love and truth are the marks of authenticity: they are what make the "real thing" the "real thing." Everything about God is real. Get in a relationship with Him. Familiarize yourself with Him. Spend time getting close to Him. Talk to Him often. Listen to what He has to say to you through His word. Make spending time with Him your priority. Experience His love for you *first*. Once you experience His love for you, then you'll have the right frame of reference for evaluating everything else that comes along. Whatever else comes along, compare it to the "real thing" and hold it up to the light so you can examine it for marks of authenticity that you know should be there (having spent time with the Real). **If you're not sure about what should be there, you're not ready for what is being presented to you.** Spend more time familiarizing yourself with Love and Light. If, on the other hand, you don't see what you *know* should be there, give that counterfeit back! You won't lose a thing!

Aleathea Dupree
Forum Administrator

FOREWORD

As usual Vikki Johnson has tapped into a critical emotional and spiritual area about which women should be educated and from which they should be liberated. Love, addiction and fallacy are a lethal combination. This triple threat continues to injure emotions and ruin relationships and relationship potential.

Love, addiction and fallacy are all formidable when engaged individually. Love is really such a small word, but so large when it is defined. Many people are on lifelong searches for that definition, to find the true meaning of love and real meaning in their love relationships. When achieved, WOW! But when it escapes your reach, reason and emotional reality, WOE! Love is a weighty matter, even when it is authentic and healthy. However, when false, or as Vikki Johnson puts it, counterfeit, it is a load that no one should choose to bear. Nevertheless, many are doing just that.

Counterfeit love by synonym is inauthentic, fake, false, feigned, fictitious, imitation, pretend, make believe and bogus, to name a few. All adjectives that describe what normally should be avoided. Yet counterfeit can seem real to the unaware and careless. When addiction is added, which supposes an internal craving combined with a loss of reason, emotional and often physical control, there you have the triple-threat combination.

These addicts can be spotted. They are the ones who have consistent relationship DNA, same guy, different name. They are the ones who continually trade the ultimate for the immediate, seized by the moment and soiled by the memory while getting further away from what they really desire. The list goes on as chronicled by this discerning author. Vikki Johnson uses her insight, experience and wisdom to expose these addicts, then to enlighten them, with the objective to emancipate them.

Addicted to Counterfeit Love is a handbook for those who seek to be rescued and freed from the phony love. It is real. It is honest. It is needed. All will again owe thanks to God and Vikki Johnson for helping them go from sickness to health in their relationships.

Bishop Derek Triplett
Hope Fellowship Church
Daytona Beach, FL

Table of Contents

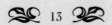

Our deepest fear is not that we are inadequate.
Our deepest fear is that we are powerful beyond measure.
It is our light, not our darkness, that most frightens us.
We ask ourselves, "Who am I to be brilliant,
gorgeous, talented, and fabulous?"
Actually, who are you not to be?
You are a child of God.
Your playing small does not serve the world.
We are all meant to shine as children do.
We were born to make manifest
the glory of God that is within us.

Marianne Williamson

Introduction

*A*re you burned out on broken relationships? External beauty without internal emotional balance is fertile ground for chaotic relationships. The good news is that there is nothing so bad that has happened in your life that God cannot fix if you just talk to Him.

Honestly, who are you not to walk in the fullness of everything God has for you? How dare you take lightly that God loves you profoundly? You are fearfully and wonderfully made to be loved with the pure essence of God Himself. You were created to love and be loved absolutely. Robin Norwood said in her book, *Women Who Love Too Much,* that loving turns into loving too much when the recipient of your love is inappropriate, uncaring or unavailable and yet you cannot walk away. In fact, you want more of their presence in your life, which leads to further dysfunction. In other words, it's easy to become addicted to emotional drama and call it love. My objective is to get you to stop protecting what you should be correcting. Why are you so committed to repeat decisions that continue to produce repeat disappointments?

Women have become so comfortable with not receiving unconditional giving, respect and honor that a lot of us now reject the "real thing" because we cannot identify it. This behavior is due to the fact that abnormal has become normal, and abnormal has also become addictive.

What is addiction? Addiction is the embracing of a behavior or thought pattern that renders one unable to make healthy choices. Often, one addiction feeds another, making it a vicious cycle.

Some women eat too much or drink too much or smoke too much. Then there are other women who have multiple addictions, including loving too much. When this happens, there is a need to address each addiction simultaneously. If not, one addiction begins to feed the other, and eventually the woman ends up in a cycle of guilt, shame, fear and powerlessness which causes her to repeat the cycle in search of a solution and in search of relief. Consequently, most women end up looking for comfort in the arms of a man, and, unfortunately, a lot of times any man will do. Why? Any man will do because the woman becomes desperate to feel loved, desirable and beautiful. Quite frequently, women use relationships for the same reason people drink alcohol, use drugs or gamble — to take the pain away.

Addicted to Counterfeit Love will uncover the destructive "love patterns" that women embrace, and guide those same women to a "love experience" — the way God intended.

This book is the result of tough love I received in the form of conversation, prayer and books I have read. Author Bill Hybels said, "Tough love chooses truth telling over peace keeping and trusts God for the outcome." For too long, we have endured unhealthy relationships built on keeping peace. Compromise never maintains lasting peace.

Counterfeit peace is worse than the greatest turmoil because it forces one to live in fear of the inevitable. An example of counterfeit peace is being afraid to be totally honest and transparent for fear of rejection or abandonment by the person you are sharing with. Consequently you agree when you really want to disagree. You lie when you really want to tell the truth. You hide when you really want to expose your innermost thoughts. Or perhaps you feel pressured to have sex because you fear not having sex will make the person no longer want to be with you.

You can't identify real love until you first understand the counterfeit. Counterfeit is a copy with the intent to defraud. We have all experienced the pain of being deceived. It does not feel good. It is an experience that is difficult to forget, destroys our capacity to trust others and is hard to get over.

Have you ever had someone say to you, "If you love me, then you will do this for me"? What about, "Of course I love you, and there is no one else"? I have been told, "No one else will want you." Have you ever been so "in love" that you ignored the warning signs of a destructive relationship? Maybe you need to be needed so you feel that you have value. Perhaps your quest is always to pursue relationships where the other person is unavailable. If you measure the depth of your love for someone by the degree of pain you are in, then you are experiencing counterfeit love, which is emotion hidden in unhealthy behaviours disguised as love.

1 John 4:7 tells us that love comes from God, and

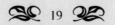

through us to others the way He intended when we fully embrace His love toward us. Verse 8 continues by saying that if you don't love others this way (God's way), then you have not become acquainted with God. You may know *of* Him, but you do not *know* Him.

The yearning and longing you feel inside you, God put there. The need for love is normal, human and spiritual. It is how we choose to respond to this desire, this wanting and this waiting that causes us conflict and pain.

We were created to relate. In Genesis 2, God said that it is not good for man to be alone. God never intended us to be alone or to live isolated lives, devoid of intimate interaction with others. God created us with the capacity for love—both to give and receive. In each of us is a longing to create a deep, intimate connection with at least one other human being. We desire affection, warmth and touch. However, this same longing seems to tease us when unfulfilled, and, therefore, makes us open to bad judgment, restlessness and impatience, which often lead to premature sexual encounters that lack intimacy.

Intimacy is a misunderstood phenomenon. Yes, intimacy is phenomenal when in the appropriate context. However, we must seek to understand the process of creating intimacy. Further, it is important to know that physical attraction that leads to casual sex without a search for deeper truth about the other person is a foundation for heartbreak. Intimacy can be encountered on many levels. Intimacy is being inside your friend (invisibly connected) and having your friend inside you. Intimacy comes from openness and self-disclosure—not by chance, but by choice. The goal of intimacy is oneness with another.

Generally, people want to love and be loved. People want to accept and be accepted. People want to connect with another person on a level where they feel secure. God designed this desire to be met in Him. We get into trouble when we seek to create this bond prematurely and outside the boundaries of marriage. Unfortunately, too many people build relationships on faulty foundations that cannot handle the weight and pressure of two people becoming one.

Genesis 2:24 says that a man will leave his father and mother and cleave to his wife, becoming one flesh. We live in a culture where we cleave to relationship after relationship after relationship, all in the name of love. It's really in the name of searching for intimacy that can only be found in God. Consequently, there are countless numbers of fractured hearts, minds, emotions and lives. This connection with another can surface on many levels with different people. The result is fragmented affection and dysfunctional capacity to enjoy a satisfying, healthy relationship with one person. Intimacy the way God intended takes place *after* a commitment is made.

Here are a few examples of connections with another person in different areas of our lives which can eventually cause pain if this bond is created before a commitment is exchanged. The thing is, God intended you to have all of these areas fulfilled in Him and then in one other person—your spouse.

There is *physical intimacy*—we become one with another because we have great sex with them. The danger of this bond is that we carry memories of this lover into our future long after the affair has ended. If you have multiple sexual partners then you have multiple memories to manage. Further, it is a known fact that when you have sex with multiple partners, and your partner has sex with multiple partners, each of you is connecting to all of the other's previous partners in the realm of the soul or emotions.

There is *spiritual intimacy*—we become one with another on a spiritual level and thus overly dependent on their spiritual capacity to nourish our God-consciousness. It can be expressed as, "I love his spirit and his relationship with God." This form of intimacy disables your ability to nurture your own relationship with God.

There is *intellectual intimacy*—we become enamored with another's intellectual capacity and "fall in love with their mind." This connection makes us vulnerable to believe whatever the other person tells us and leaves us open to be easily persuaded.

There is *recreational intimacy*—we connect with another to have fun, attend social gatherings and simply hang out. Women often mistake this investment of time as love and it's not. You are just a "buddy" and your willingness to participate gives him someone to hang out with without the drama or responsibility of a commitment.

There is *crisis intimacy*—we grow to depend on another emotionally because they were there for us during a difficult period. We interpret their support as an eternal connection, and, quite frequently, it was just support for a certain time. This attachment can be hard to break because often the other person's presence has a calming or soothing effect.

There is *creative intimacy*—we feel a deep bond with

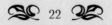

someone because we are very productive when they are around. "We were meant to be together because we are good together." Not necessarily so in most cases.

There is *communication intimacy*—we grow fond of someone because we can talk to them about anything at any time. Many extramarital affairs are launched from this premature place of intimacy. Quite often, the more intense the conversation, the more intense the attraction can become. This is also the power of online dating and social Web sites.

There is *familial intimacy*—we connect with someone because our family loves them and their family loves us. The familiarity is what fertilizes this premature bond. Guess what? You're not going to marry the family. Pay attention to your partner *and* to how your partner relates to your family.

Then there is *emotional intimacy*—we give more of ourselves than a wholesome friendship requires. Emotional intimacy has a hold on you when you are longing for "more" and there is no movement in the direction of a commitment. Emotional intimacy produces an intense attachment to another person. Sometimes, it can render one unable to function because the pain of being disconnected from someone you are emotionally attached to literally robs your energy and strength.

We often look for all these needs to be met in one person, and, unfortunately, that all-sufficient person does *not* exist. The truth is, these needs require multiple healthy relationships and friendships in addition to an intimate relationship with Jesus Christ. So if you are one of those people who proudly proclaims, "I don't have any friends," you are really declaring, "I lack intimacy in my life." You are also revealing that you are a loner (almost always due to past trauma) and that your relational skills are oppressed.

Why do you constantly seek escape from the thing you crave rather than take the risk of relating to others? I'll answer that for you—fear! In true friendship, there is no holding back. Thus, we need the wisdom of God to select true friends because this type of intimacy is costly, but it produces dividends of joy. The Bible says in Proverbs 27:6 "Faithful are the wounds of a friend." True friendship loves you enough to be honest with you—even at the risk of losing the relationship.

Love the way God intended is more than an emotion. It is an act of the will, thoughts and emotions that must be in harmony for the relationship to be healthy. It is impossible to relate to others in a wholesome manner if you can't relate to yourself with honesty. You cannot give away what you do not possess. By the time you finish this encounter with truth, you will be on the pathway to loving God, loving self and loving others the way God designed.

Jennifer's Story

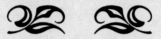

CAN'T LET GO
(The Past)

Jennifer is stuck. Even though she continues to meet new people, she can't get over the betrayal of her last relationship and the one before that and the one before that. At some point, she always finds a way to sabotage a good thing. It doesn't matter if it is a friendship with another female or a potentially romantic relationship with a nice guy. "Every time someone tries to help me I seem to push them away. What is wrong with me?" she wonders to herself.

Jennifer wasn't betrayed. The reality is that she feels betrayed whenever she can't control the other person or have her way. At that point, she becomes mean-spirited, combative, insecure and hard to get along with. She is critical of everything and everybody that she comes in contact with. Eventually, people get tired of Jennifer's tirades and accusations. They stop calling or taking her calls. "Am I always going to be this way?" she asks herself over and over.

Her behavior is really the result of a traumatic childhood. You see, Jennifer is an only child who grew up with an alcoholic mother. When Jennifer was twelve, her mother left to go to the liquor store one evening and never came back home. After two days of being alone, hungry and missing school, Jennifer finally told a neighbor what was going on. Mrs. Jackson, an elderly woman who lived with her three cats, gave Jennifer something to eat. Then she called the police. That was the beginning of Jennifer's life in foster care.

Now that Jennifer is twenty-four and trying to move on with her life after coming out of drug rehab, it's starting to become painfully clear why she pushes people away when they start to get close. She compares everyone to her mother and believes wholeheartedly that if her own mother walked away from her, then everyone else will do the same.

When you are consumed by the past, you mismanage your present and cripple your future with skill gaps— especially regarding relationships. The more difficult it is to end a relationship that is bad for you, the more elements of the childhood struggle it contains. However, you must understand that letting go does not mean that you stop caring.

When you are stuck in destructive behavior, it is because you are trying to overcome pain from your childhood and to find relief from a wrong you have experienced. It is sometimes hard to break away from negative thinking. It can be etched deep in the subconscious. Love doesn't leave. But then again, it is impossible to have love leave if love was never there in the first place.

We all have felt anger at one time or another. Anger can range from mild irritation to intense fury and rage. Like other emotions, it is accompanied by physiological and biological changes. For example, when you get angry your heart rate increases and your blood pressure goes up. The instinctive, natural way to express anger is to respond aggressively. Anger is a natural response to threats and can inspire powerful aggressive feelings. In other words, to a certain extent, anger is necessary for survival. However, unexpressed anger can create other problems—namely unforgiveness.

Unforgiveness is a silent killer! Unforgiveness drags the offender into your future. Anger is deceptive and keeps you from thinking clearly. Anger is also a natural response to disappointment. Anger blinds you. It is poison that hinders progress and blocks you from receiving blessings that are headed your way. Whatever we feed grows and whatever we starve eventually dies. Whatever you don't forgive, you will relive.

This mindset causes you to strike out at others and to be very critical, and it robs you of the joy of loving and being loved in return. Author Bob Gass said, "Unforgiveness is an umbilical cord that keeps you tied to the past. When you forgive, you cut the cord. When you refuse to forgive, you remain tied to memories that can affect you endlessly." Author and counselor John Mason said, "Unforgiveness is the one guaranteed formula for smothering our originality. A poor memory is your best response to being wronged. Never carry a grudge. It only affects you." You can't get ahead while trying to get even. Unforgiveness does a great deal more damage to the vessel in which it is stored than to the object on which it is being poured.

We all know the importance of maintaining good health. Daily we are surrounded with reminders to eat right, exercise and be well so we can do well. We hear the messages. But do we really process the information? We get regular checkups to manage our overall health. We get our eyes examined and visit our dentist twice a year. We have exercise routines; perhaps go to the gym, and if we don't, we have videos, DVDs, books, posters and magazines on exercise plans. Some of us may even have treadmills in our homes and other workout equipment to keep our bodies in shape. We try to eat the right things and drink plenty of water…or at least we should.

What about our ability to forgive quickly? This checkup is just as important, if not more so. We must do a forgiveness check on ourselves every now and then. Did you know that negative emotion transforms itself into negative energy or deadly toxins that can manifest as sickness and disease? Unforgiveness is the cause of ailments such as stress, high blood pressure, cancer, depression, insomnia, bitterness, resentment, hatred, overeating, undereating—the list could go on and on.

Our self-esteem levels are connected to our ability to forgive quickly. Don't give anyone or anything that power over you. Unforgiveness will zap your power to effectively move forward and will result in unwanted emotional baggage. Stop living your life more connected to your hurt than to your healing.

You are reading this book because God wants to challenge the weak spots in your life. God wants to effect change for the better in your life. Stop using worldly judgments to view yourself. I have found that people do not inherently resist change as much as they resist loss or the sacrifice required to change. You hold the key to happiness, joy, peace, contentment, laughter and success. It is found in the ability to forgive yourself quickly and then release yourself from the bondage of emotional torment that surrounds this ugly, crippling behavior. At the end of the day forgiveness heals and changes how we remember.

Life Lessons Learned In This Chapter

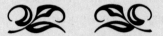

WHEN LOVE SETS YOU FREE YOU ARE FREE INDEED

- When you are consumed by your past, you mismanage your present.
- Unexpressed anger always results in unforgiveness.
- Unforgiveness is a silent killer.
- Unforgiveness zaps your power to effectively move on with your life.
- Forgiveness heals and changes how we remember.

Scripture

Whenever you pray, if you have anything against anyone, forgive him that your Father in heaven may also forgive you your trespasses. But if you do not forgive, neither will your Father in heaven forgive your trespasses.

Mark 11:25-26

Written Affirmation

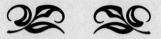

Share Your Thoughts

I will not live my life stuck in the past and I choose to release any unforgiveness because:

_____

_____

_____

_____

_____

_____

_____

CeeCee's Story

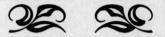

THERE IS NO WE — IT'S JUST YOU
(Fantasy)

CeeCee and Tavis met at the bowling alley about three months ago. CeeCee was there with some girlfriends celebrating her best friend's birthday. Tavis was usually there on Fridays because he was in a bowling league. Their chance meeting at the snack bar interrupted CeeCee's otherwise pretty boring life. Tavis accidentally knocked over CeeCee's soda while reaching for a napkin and that's how her dream relationship began.

Unfortunately, that's not how is ended. Tavis bought her another soda, apologized every time he saw her that night, and on the way out after he had finished bowling, flashed the most beautiful smile she had ever seen. "Wait a minute," she shouted as she ran toward the front entrance. "At least you can give me your phone number so I can call you every time I think about that soda I never got to drink." Tavis gave her his number and said, "I'll do my best to keep in touch. I travel quite a bit for my job, but I always manage to get back home for my Friday-night bowling."

Little did Tavis know that CeeCee meant exactly what she said. The next day she called him around lunchtime to let him know she had just thought about her spilled soda. Tavis was a good sport, laughed it off and, after a few minutes of small talk, ended the conversation. CeeCee thought, "Gosh, I love his voice. This is going to be the relationship of my dreams."

Over the next several weeks, CeeCee called Tavis every day. For some reason, she never thought it was strange that he didn't call her—ever. Maybe he needs to see me again before he asks me to be his lady, she thought. So CeeCee started making excuses to show up at the bowling alley on Friday nights when she knew Tavis would be there for his league. He was a perfect gentleman. He always spoke to CeeCee but never made any moves the way a man would if he was interested in pursuing a relationship.

Two Friday nights later, CeeCee understood why her dream relationship with Tavis had never materialized. As she walked into the bowling alley, she saw Tavis sharing a tender moment with one of his team members. CeeCee was crushed. Tavis's moment wasn't with a woman, it was with a man. In that moment CeeCee realized that it wasn't just that he wasn't into her, Tavis wasn't into women period.

> There is no you and me—it's just you
> We are not having a thing—it's just you
> Your mind is telling you something that isn't true
> It's time for you to stop letting your feelings lie to you
> There is no you and me—it's just you.

(lyrics used by permission 3Dtrip, LLC)

I remember when I was in elementary school my favorite flowers to pick were flowers with a lot of petals. I would daydream about the cute boy I was in "puppy love" with at the time and recite the little phrase, "He loves me, he loves me not," until the last petal remained. My next action was based on the last petal left on the flower. If my little game ended with "he loves me not," I would find another cute boy deserving of my daydream. Those were the rules I played by.

Then I matriculated to middle school and the process of selecting who was worthy of my affection became more intense. Most of the time, it was the popular boy that the other girls were also excited about. I would sit in class and, instead of listening to my teacher, I would practice the signature of my new last name. I would lie outside and stare at the sky, daydreaming about how popular I was going to be once the popular boy picked me as his favorite.

In high school this fantasy role-playing went to another level. Now I had the names of my children, the color of my bridesmaids' dresses, the location of my honeymoon and the songs that would be sung on my wedding day. Oh yes, I could even describe my wedding dress. Now all I needed was a groom to plug into the elaborate plans of my fantasy.

Several boys came and went as I grew into a woman. For the most part, my relationships were cool. I learned so much with each new experience. Quite often, after being in the relationship for a few months, I would discover that I was more into the "relationship thing" than he was. I thought I was in love while he was in ego heaven.

Boys will be boys when girls don't understand their own value and self-worth. In some cases, by the time my guy realized how special I was, I was no longer interested in him to the same degree.

Attraction and infatuation are powerful emotions. This rush or feeling of being high sends our imaginations into overdrive. We start daydreaming about what our kids will look like, where we'll build our dream house and how being around this man just makes us happy no matter what's going on in our lives. I remember a song with lyrics that basically said, if you are not in my life I will die. How many times have we felt that we could not live without that special someone? That's what I thought—too many times to count—and I'm still here. Anyone who renders us this helpless and dysfunctional has too much power. It's a terrible thing to be in an unreciprocated relationship.

Falling in love, being in love, staying in love with someone who does not feel the same way about you is a very damaging experience. The power of this nugget is in the preposition. There's a tremendous difference between being "in love" and making a commitment and a choice "to love." Making a commitment "to love" is based on daily help. We need God's grace, courage, wisdom, and the agreement of mind, will and emotions to honor a commitment to love on a daily basis. The question is, can we commit to love each other—even when the "high" dissipates?

However, many of us continue to daydream, plan and live with an agenda that we alone created. Consequently, we pick the wrong guy to overwhelm with information about our plans, and before we know it, he's gone. He does not call anymore. You have a chance meeting on the street and his awkward smile tells you that he is unpleasantly surprised to see you. He promises to call you and never does. When you call and leave him voice-mail messages, he never returns the calls or acknowledges that he even listened to them.

In the end, we are left devastated because all along, we have been in this relationship alone. Let me share a secret with you, ladies. The relationship is what the man says it is. This is a harsh reality and you cannot make someone love you.

Life Lessons Learned In This Chapter

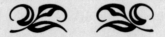

LOVE IS NOT BLIND—LOVE SEES VERY CLEARLY

- Attraction and infatuation are powerful emotions.
- Being in love with someone who does not feel the same is a damaging experience.
- There is a tremendous difference between being "in love" and making a commitment "to love."
- Ladies—the relationship is what the man says it is.

Scripture

The Lord will perfect that which concerns me.

Psalms 138:8

Written Affirmation

Share Your Thoughts

I choose to relate to the opposite sex with a realistic, God-driven perspective because:

_____

_____

_____

_____

_____

_____

_____

Emily's Story

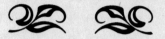

SHOW ME YOU LOVE ME
(Sex)

*R*olando was thirty-five years old, six foot five and two hundred and forty-five pounds of milk-chocolate fineness that every woman daydreams about. From his Armani suits to his perfect bald head to that beautiful black Range Rover he parks in the garage, he was certainly going to be a great catch for the right woman. He was a CPA with one of the largest accounting firms in Detroit.

Emily was an executive assistant at a law firm in the same building. She loved her new job and couldn't believe she landed such a gig after being in Detroit only two weeks. Emily had just relocated to Detroit from Farmington, Pennsylvania, because she wanted to experience life in the big city. She'd also grown tired of the same ol' small-town guys who were always trying to engage her in small talk. After months of research, she decided to move to the Motor City.

After seeing each other in the elevator morning after morning and greeting one another with a cordial good morning, Rolando decided to step up to the plate and ask Emily to lunch. Emily was a looker herself. She was five foot six, with an athletic build and sandy-blond locks and hazel eyes that could cast a spell on you. Emily agreed to lunch that day and so "it" began. From that day on, they ate lunch together at least three days a week, and eventually they started having dinner together, too. Dinner quickly progressed to spending the night and having sex. If it was a night when they didn't have dinner, it became normal for Rolando to call Emily after eleven o'clock, inviting her over to his place for "a little late-night fun." It just seemed like a natural progression in her mind.

About three months into this casual friendship, Rolando invited Emily to go away with him for the weekend to his fraternity golf gathering. Without hesitation, Emily agreed, and it was off to Canada for more "private time" with "her man." Certainly he couldn't be involved with anyone else because he spends most of his time with me. I know he's going to pop the question soon. Why else would he invite me to go away with him to spend time with his friends? Emily pondered. Unfortunately, when they arrived at the resort, Emily found out why he'd invited her. It was a fraternity get-together all right and golf was available for those who wanted to play. But more than that, Emily found out that Rolando was a ladies' man. Woman after woman after woman greeted him as they made their way to their room. One of his frat brothers walked by and, with a boyish grin, punched Rolando on the arm and said, "Brought some new ladies for the weekend, huh, bro?" Emily's heart sank.

I believe that the Bible is the infallible Word of God. I am sharing that to lay the foundation for a very popular subject discussed in books, on the radio, on television, in the movies and which at one point or another, affects all of our lives. Let's talk about sex! Sex is a wonderful and beautiful experience designed by God to be enjoyed in the context of marriage. Hebrews 13:4 says, "Marriage is honorable among all, and the bed undefiled; but fornicators and adulterers God will judge." In other words, sex outside of marriage is wrong.

In this chapter, I am not promoting sex outside of marriage. However, since so many people enter into these types of relationships, I am addressing the psychological and emotional damage caused by this type of encounter that so many women confuse with love.

Sex is not a builder of relationships. Sex is not love. Sex is the ultimate privilege of the one, God-ordained relationship where sex is divinely allowed—marriage between a man and a woman. Tina Turner asked, "What's love got to do with it?" Love has everything to do with sex the way God intended. When a relationship involves sex only, it's like having in your possession the number-one single that you heard on the radio without having the enjoyment of the entire CD. Eventually you get tired of hearing the same song over and over and over again—even when it's an artist that you really like. A sex-only relationship is like brushing your teeth without toothpaste—going through the motions without the lasting benefit. Sex without love is like eating a slice of pizza without the cheese—the main ingredient holding the other ingredients together. Yes, it was pizza but it was boring, tough to deal with after a while because all the good stuff kept falling apart, and while it may have been filling, it was not fulfilling or satisfying at all.

Most men will not refuse sex. Women need a reason for sex. Men use sex as a release. Men need a place—that's it. At the same time, most men want to pursue or hunt the woman they want to have meaningful, passionate sex with…like a wife! Once sex enters a relationship, everything is centered around the sex. You go to dinner as a prelude to sex. You catch a late movie as a precursor to sex. You go away on vacation, enjoy the sights, go back to your hotel room and have sex. Sex does not necessarily take the relationship to another level. It's just sex.

In addition to sexually transmitted diseases, unwanted pregnancies and broken hearts, sex (in the name of love) outside of marriage produces an "emotional tsunami" that eventually washes over the essence of who you are as a woman. How many times have you heard of a woman losing her mind after she entered a sex-only relationship? She begins to exhibit insane behavior such as paranoia, confronting those she suspects of being the other women, hiring private investigators or becoming a self-trained private investigator herself, going through her man's belongings looking for evidence of someone else. In other words, the woman's life is turned upside down with drama and for what? Her life is turned upside down for sex in the name of love.

Your soul, which is the seat of your emotions, is connected to your sexuality. A man cannot touch your body without touching your emotions. This makes you vulnerable and open to begin tolerating behavior you would not normally deal with from a man because now you are driven purely by your emotions instead of by your mind, will and emotions. When you feel you have to give sex to get love, the relationship is destined to fail. Sex outside of marriage creates mistrust, because it clouds your judgment. Premature sex produces pain, loneliness, guilt, morning-after regret, feelings of betrayal, jealousy and insecurity. Stop being a dumping ground! Sexual intercourse as a means to vent frustration is not making love at all. It is a release of pent-up energy.

Sometimes, the deception of sex outside of marriage can lead to "playing house." The sex is good, you enjoy each other's company, your families interact and you may even have children together. However, if you are not married, it is not real love. It is a fractured representation of God's intention for man and woman, which is marriage. Many women are involved in the playing-house type of relationship. A great majority are living in silent frustration because their partner will not commit to marriage. Consequently, they get caught in this situation for what can easily become years waiting for the ultimate commitment that will never come.

If he loves you so much then why won't he marry you? Why go through the motions of marriage with no legal benefits? Love commits. If he is not ready to get married to you, then he is not ready to be responsible for your emotions, your well-being, your present and your future. The person who is willing to protect *all* of you is the person who has the divine right to *enjoy* all of you.

Paula Rinehart says in her book, *Sex and the Soul of a*

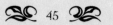

Woman, that allowing a man to enjoy sexual favors without having to take the risk of real commitment in marriage invites him to remain a boy inside. Men are on their best behavior while in pursuit. However, once sex outside of marriage takes place, in most cases, the romance is over. He should pursue your heart before he pursues your body.

I know what you're thinking: He will marry me — eventually. I understand that you wash his clothes, clean his house, take care of his children and you just want to keep him happy. I understand that you don't want to pressure him to get married — or get married again since he has only been divorced for five years. I understand that you believe that by allowing him to do whatever he wants to do with whomever he wants to do it with he will appreciate the freedom you give him.

Pam Stenzel, author of *Sex Has a Price Tag,* says there isn't a condom in the world that will protect your heart. If you take the emotions out of sex, then you are just animals acting out biological urges. Sex outside of marriage has consequences — no matter what. Sex binds you and sex blinds you when it takes place outside the marriage relationship. Getting over a sex-only relationship takes twice the amount of time that the relationship itself lasted.

How many morning-after stories of regret do you have? Sometimes regret doesn't wait until the next morning but hits you in the midst of the sex act. How crazy is that? It's insane to keep volunteering for the same miserable experience over and over again. How many times have you given in to sex outside of marriage when you really wanted to say no? God's intent is that we be a man's sweetheart, not his sex depot!

You are loved by God. Who else do you need to impress? Make your life an experiment of living in the love of God. Don't throw your self-esteem away on things and people that don't matter. Love is a choice, not a mood, a magic feeling or a reaction, but a choice.

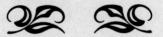

<u>GREAT SEX DOES NOT EQUAL GREAT LOVE</u>

- Sex is not a builder of relationships.
- Sex is not love.
- Most men will not refuse sex.
- Women need a reason for sex. Men need a place.
- Getting over a sex-only relationship takes twice the amount of time that the relationship itself lasted.

Scripture

For this reason I also suffer these things; nevertheless I am not ashamed, for I know whom I have believed and am persuaded that He is able to keep what I have committed to Him until that Day.

2 Timothy 1:12

Written Affirmation

Share Your Thoughts

I will not have casual sex while looking for true love because:

_____

_____

_____

_____

_____

_____

_____

Allison's Story

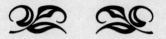

YOU NEED ME
(Codependency)

Allison and Jake had been together for two years. Their relationship was strange to most people, including Allison and Jake. It worked for them, however, so they felt no real need to change anything.

Allison worked at the local grocery store as general manager, and she also had a side job as a manicurist in her friend's hair salon. On average, Allison worked six days a week, approximately fifteen hours a day. It took both incomes for her to afford her two-bedroom apartment just outside St. Louis, pay her car loan and her insurance. Jake had been unemployed for the last six months and in the midst of "looking for another job," had had his car repossessed, lost his apartment because he could no longer afford to pay rent, and lost all the furniture that he was leasing from the local furniture-rental store. Instead of offering to pay his rent for him as she had done so many times before, Allison convinced Jake to come and live with her temporarily. That should be easy enough, he thought. Heck, all he had to move was his clothes and his computer game gear. Of course, he agreed and promised to have a new job in the next few days.

The next few days turned into weeks, and now it has been months since Jake has received a paycheck. He didn't have any unemployment to collect because he used it all up the last time he was unemployed.

Jake had it made. He took Allison to work most days and kept her car. His daily routine consisted of dropping Allison at the store, then he would stop by the barber shop to hang out with his boys for a few hours before he returned to Allison's place, no, "their" place, to fix some lunch. After lunch he would take a nap, spend a few hours playing video games and then be ready to look through the job opportunities that Allison had printed off the Internet the night before. For some reason, he just could not seem to find a job that he would enjoy. Jake was late almost every day picking Allison up from work and thought nothing of it. In her heart, Allison was feeling used, but she loved Jake and didn't want to put unnecessary pressure on him. So she continued to help him the best way she knew how. She put her feelings of resentment aside and convinced herself that things would get better soon.

$\mathcal{M}$any people have characteristics of codependent behavior. Some recognize it but most don't. Codependency is quite common in those who come from dysfunctional families as well as in children whose parents were alcoholics and/or addicts.

Based on divorce statistics today, the number of people coming from dysfunctional families is quite large. It follows then that our society is dealing with clusters of people who tend to focus on everyone else's feelings, actions and words and to neglect themselves.

The codependent personality is often a rescuer constantly trying to save others from the consequences they are about to face. Most of the time the codependent fails at this rescue attempt, enabling the individual they are trying to rescue to continue making the poor choices that they are experiencing. The consequence of this behavior is that everyone is frustrated, no one is making progress, each person has trouble maintaining "meaningful" relationships, and ultimately each person is unable to trust their own feelings.

Who can I fix today? Your need to be needed is simply creating more problems that need correcting. "I'm using my gift to help," is what you tell yourself. You were not born this way. You learned this behavior and consequently, you can unlearn it.

Codependence, according to the Mental Health Association, is an emotional and behavioral condition that affects an individual's ability to have a healthy, mutually satisfying relationship. These relationships are characterized by some or a combination of the following:

- An exaggerated sense of responsibility for other's actions
- No clear boundaries
- A tendency to confuse love and pity, with the tendency to "love" people they can pity and rescue
- A tendency to do more than your share and then resent it
- Difficulty adjusting to change
- Difficulty making decisions
- An unhealthy dependence on relationships
- Difficulty letting go
- Denying, minimizing, or altering how you truly feel
- A tendency to perceive oneself as totally unselfish
- A tendency to compromise one's values and integrity to avoid rejection or another's anger
- A tendency to put aside one's interests to do what others want

Codependence is a deeply rooted compulsive behavior born out of moderately to extremely dysfunctional family systems. We have each experienced in our own ways the painful trauma of the emptiness of our childhood and relationships throughout our lives.

A codependent will attempt to use others as a sole source of identity, value and well-being, and as a way of trying to restore the emotional losses from a low-nurturance childhood which has caused fluctuating inner pain. Codependents imply, plead, whine, demand, are aggressive, threatening, and often portray themselves as the victim in relationships. Codependents consistently violate their integrity every time they do something that goes

against their key, core values. Codependent people have good intentions, they just use faulty execution.

Basically, the only person you can control is yourself. Be true to who you are and ultimately, you will become effective in the lives of others.

Life Lessons Learned In This Chapter

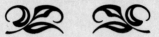

<u>LOVE COVERS (PROTECTS) WHILE IT CORRECTS</u>

- Codependent people like to rescue others to feel good about themselves.
- Codependent people have difficulty letting go.
- Codependent people have a hard time adjusting to change.
- Codependent people have an exaggerated sense of responsibility for others' actions.

Scripture

Let not mercy and truth forsake you; Bind them around your neck, write them on the tablet of your heart, and so find favor and high esteem in the sight of God and man.

Proverbs 3:3

Written Affirmation

Share Your Thoughts

I will not participate in codependent relationships because:

_____

_____

_____

_____

_____

_____

_____

Katie's Story

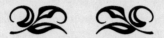

WHAT ARE WE DOING?
(Undefined Relationships)

Katie was in Chicago for a business trip. She and her coworkers were attending a staff dinner at one of the fabulous restaurants along the Magnificent Mile. The menu was amazing, the jazz music was soothing and the men were gorgeous. "I must have died and gone to heaven," Katie said to Tina, her shy and quiet associate. Katie excused herself to go to the ladies' room and literally bumped into Joshua St. James, an old flame from years ago. He still looked good and still had the most mesmerizing smile of any man she had ever met.

In that moment, she flashed back to the year they were "hanging out" together. They talked several times a day, prayed together, supported each other's events and were the joy of each other's family. Their conversations and interaction had led Katie to believe that Joshua was "her man" and she was "his woman," until she received an e-mail from her cousin asking her if she and Joshua were still together. "Yes, of course. Why would you ask me that?" was the response she returned to her cousin via e-mail. The next e-mail knocked the wind out of

Katie. It was a newspaper picture of Joshua and another woman taken recently in New York. The two looked quite cozy and when she asked Joshua about the photo, he brushed it off saying it was really nothing. He said the woman was a client and that he was just her escort for the evening. Katie let it go at that.

Several weeks later, Katie was preparing for another business trip and thought back to the question her cousin had asked. "Are you and Joshua still together?" For some reason, this time she evaluated their connection differently. He had never really asked her to be his lady. He had never introduced her as his lady. While he was open to sharing information about his life, Joshua never gave Katie specific details. "Are we together at all? What are we doing?" Katie wondered. No longer would she just go through the motions and "see where things went."

She picked up the phone, called Joshua and flat-out asked him, "What are we doing? What is this?" His initial silence spoke volumes. Obviously, he was thinking how he should respond. "Katie, I am enjoying what I thought was a great friendship. I'm just not ready to be in a fully committed relationship with anyone," was his reply. "That's all I needed to hear, Joshua, because moving forward, I want to be very clear on us," Katie said. That conversation had been four years ago. That was the last time they'd spoken—until now.

$\mathcal{M}$en and women view relationships differently. I have learned that men make wonderful friends and confidants. Just because a relationship does not work romantically does not mean you throw away the potential of a friendship. It is critical to be authentic and honest from the beginning, because eventually we attract into our lives who we are.

A successful friendship is based on what each person brings to the relationship. Some of my most important friendships are with men. We share mutual appreciation, trust and trustworthiness. We enjoy caring, supportive and nurturing conversation, companionship, and are deeply committed to each other's well-being on a non-sexual, non-romantic level. It is friendship of the ultimate kind. However, too many times women skip over the stages of "getting to know you," only to arrive prematurely at the dangerous stage of desiring and expecting long-term commitment based on short-term knowledge.

The key to a healthy male/female friendship is *clear communication*. Communication is a two-way exchange of thoughts, messages or signals. This involves words, listening, body language, perceptions, assumptions, interpretations, evaluations and examination. What is he saying? What are you saying? What is his response? What is your response? Are you hearing what you want to hear or are you hearing exactly what he said? Are you his buddy? Are you his friend with benefits? Are you his confidante?

He said, "Let's take our time and get to know each other." You heard, "In a week we will know each other well enough to commit to one another." He meant, let's take our time and get to know each other because you might be a crazy, bipolar, neurotic female.

He said, "I've never met a woman like you before." You heard, "Ah-hah, I will be his wife because I know he hasn't said that to anyone else. He just told me so." He meant that he has never met anyone like you before because he hasn't.

He said, "I don't have the capacity for someone special in my life right now." You heard, "He just hasn't met anyone like me, but once he experiences me he will create the space." He meant, If you are going to pressure me into your false expectations we can stop right now, because I don't have time, energy or space for more drama in my life.

He said, "I'm not ready for a committed relationship because I just came out of one and I need to work on me." You heard, "His ex was a witch and really hurt him. I'll fix him right up so he can be what I need to survive. I have nothing but time." He meant, I am not committing to you or anyone else at this time because I want to enjoy my freedom and recover from the chaos I have endured for the last several years.

He said, "I'm open to seeing where this goes." You heard, "I must be the one for him." He meant, As long as you don't pressure me into a commitment, I'm going to get as much as I can as long as I can unless someone more interesting and intriguing comes along and takes your place.

My point is that you must establish a clear destination before departure. Otherwise, you will just be going around in circles, headed nowhere very, very fast. Basically, if you don't clearly establish the boundaries of the relationship, it is a waste of time, energy, gasoline, money and emotion.

A friend shared with me that often there is a divide between what we as women anticipate and what they (the men) have planned. In these types of relationships, men often take advantage of whatever the woman offers, particularly if there is no demand placed on them to define the relationship. They will accept your gifts, eat your delicious meals, let you clean their houses, wash their clothes, support their dreams, patronize their businesses, use your ideas, escort you to functions, visit your church, attend your family gatherings, and all without the promise of a future because, in their minds, they have never made a commitment to you.

I don't care how cute, smart or witty you are, if he does not verbally express his intent to commit, *he is not interested in committing!* Don't define your relationship by his actions alone. Don't misinterpret him calling you often for him missing you. Don't mistake him enjoying your company at dinner for him wanting to spend the rest of his life with you. Listen to what he says and see if his words and actions are in agreement. The moment you begin hinting around that you want more, the drama and the inner dread begins. A man is very clear when he wants more. I am not referring to more benefits (sex) without a commitment, either.

Let's take a look at why people enter these types of relationships. Some people are very deceptive and want to enjoy as many benefits as possible before a demand is placed on them to commit. They are just selfish. Others take advantage of the power they know they have over the other person with no intention of moving forward in the relationship.

Some non-deceptive reasons people enter these types of relationships include ignorance of their own intentions, feelings and capacities (or space) for this type of emotional connection. In other words, they just blindly "go with the flow" until something different happens or a demand is placed on them. Another reason people find temporary solace in this type of relationship might be an injury from a previous relationship. An undefined relationship is safe, because the person knows they are not healed enough to enter another committed relationship.

Potential hurts or disadvantages of this type of relationship are: (1) emotional devastation, including feelings of betrayal, anger or bitterness, (2) mental torment including confusion, misunderstanding or depression, (3) physical ailments, including stress, anxiety or panic attacks, ulcers, migraines or eating disorders, (4) missing out, meaning the person's intentions remain nebulous for so long that the other person moves on, tired of waiting for the relationship to be defined. It is best to keep sex out of undefined relationships so the relationship is not defined by default.

Human nature is such that we value what we have to pay a price for. The greater the price, the greater the care we tend to use in protecting our investment. Take your life off Pause and push Play. Let him catch up with you and clearly define his intentions.

Ladies be very clear on this—you are the prize! If he wants to pay the cost, then he can have some of your precious time. If not, then I'll share a quote from a

coworker that literally changed how I view reciprocity in relationships: "Never allow someone to be your priority while for them, you are just an option." Enough said!

Life Lessons Learned In This Chapter

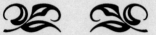

<u>LOVE DOES NOT PLAY WITH YOUR EMOTIONS</u>

- Men and women view relationships differently.
- Successful friendship is based on what each person brings to the relationship.
- The key to healthy male/female friendship is clear communication.
- Men value what they have to pay for.

Scripture

Guard your heart with all diligence, for out of it flows the issues of life.

Proverbs 4:23

Written Affirmation

Share Your Thoughts

Though I may have done so in the past, I will no longer settle for undefined relationships because:

_____

_____

_____

_____

_____

_____

_____

Michelle's Story

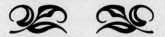

YOU ARE NOT HIS MOTHER
(Over-nurturing)

"*Ronald, please stop leaving your clothes all over the floor!*" screamed Michelle as she walked through the pile of dirty clothes, picking them up.

Michelle and Ronald have been married for six years now. From the time they got together, Michelle has always been around to fix whatever is wrong in Ronald's life. She dislikes who he dislikes. She likes who he likes. She covers for him when the creditors call. She lies to his job when she calls in sick for him so he can take a day off. She cooks his breakfast, lunch and dinner and insists that he always eat his vegetables. She balances his checking account to make sure that his child-support payments to his two baby mamas are paid on time. At all costs, she intervenes so that Ronald does not have to feel the pain of the consequences of his bad choices.

Every now and then she catches herself talking down to him as if he is her child. That's natural because, for the most part, he feels like her child and, at times, he acts like her child. Little does Michelle know that her constant ranting and smothering is driving a wedge between them. Ronald has begun to feel as though Michelle no longer respects him and, for the most part, he is right. The reason she tolerates Ronald's behavior is because she is used to it, and she doesn't want to be alone. "If I just hang in here with Ronald, eventually he will change and be the husband I always thought he could be. However, he can't do it without my help. He needs me to stay around so that when things go wrong I can fix what's broken and I can heal what's hurting. That's what women do, right?"

In our hip-hop culture today, young men refer to beautiful women as "Ma" or "Mommy" as a compliment. That's *not* what this chapter is about. We grew up watching many types of mothers on television. Depending on your age you may have watched June Cleaver, who kept everything together and always responded with a "Yes, dear." Or maybe you are familiar with Carol Brady, who managed to keep up with six kids, supervise her housekeeper, Alice, and was, miraculously, always happy to see her husband no matter how her day had gone. Perhaps Florida Evans from *Good Times* was your favorite TV mom as she let James know exactly what was on her mind. Even though they moved on up to the East Side, Louise Jefferson was not a slouch either. She was an equal partner in the relationship.

Each of these TV moms in some way or another "mothered" their men. The key words here are *TV mom*. Nothing good can come out of this type of interaction if the man is not your son. A woman should not be filling out job applications for a man and mailing them off. A woman should not be signing him up for classes. A woman should not be coming home to clean and cook for him even though he is unemployed, not looking for employment and home watching television all day.

The key to a positive relationship is balance. A lot of women make the mistake of mothering instead of letting the man be independently macho. You know, like when he refuses to ask for directions when he is driving and lost. Instead of becoming frustrated and irritated and yelling like his mom would do, simply pull out that steamy paperback you've been longing to get into and start reading with a smile.

A needy man will be fine with you while he is down. The moment he gets back on his feet you will become annoying to him. A man who wants a woman to take care of him will begin to take you for granted and will eventually become more of a burden than a blessing.

Do you have a compulsion to nurture? Let's start by evaluating you:

- Do you need to fix his problems?
- Do you clean up behind him as though he is an invalid?
- Do you intervene and help him avoid responsibility?
- Do you protect him from consequences?
- Do you feel connected to him when he shares his drama-filled life with you?
- Do you kick into gear to mend all his broken places?
- Do you listen to countless hours of his self-pity?
- Do you pay for everything (dinner, gas, clothes, recreation) so he won't feel pressured?
- Do you feel yourself wanting to take care of him?
- Do you thrive on his "I don't care," "No one will help me," "I can't make it," "If only I could get a break," "They've done me wrong" soliloquies?
- Do you talk to your man as if he is your son?

This is not love. I realize that some men's behavior stems from how they were raised by their mothers. Many mothers still pamper their adult sons to the point of creating skill gaps and consequently, inadequate life skills.

However, for you to participate in the continued dysfunction is insanity. You are contributing to the retarded development of your man. Break free from this cycle of mothering your man. He is an adult and life happens. Obstacles, challenges and problems are a part of life. You are depriving yourself of the wonderful joy of experiencing a healthy, edifying relationship. Allow him to be irritated to greatness. Your role is not to fix his discomfort when those types of situations are intended for his growth. If he has not learned to manage life, he can't manage a relationship either.

Be proactive. Many women get blinded by a handsome man in a nice suit, driving a nice car, flashing a nice smile. Don't be so consumed with biceps and a six-pack that you overlook his intellectual capacity and emotional maturity or immaturity. Pay attention to the constant complaints about his job, his siblings, baby-mama drama, money issues, and his everyone-else-is-always-wrong song. Pay attention to bright-red flags that are flying around in every conversation. Obviously, he wants you or someone to fix it all. He wants you to rescue him from all the dysfunction that surrounds his very existence. If a man refuses to grow up, accept responsibilities and act like an adult, **run—don't walk—away!!**

If you can't get away because you are already married to him, then my advice to you is to be his wife, not his mother. Stop talking to your man as if he is your child. Your power is in your gentle, feminine ways, not your ranting, yelling and screaming. Ask God for grace to endure the inconvenient times if it means your husband learns the lessons of the responsibilities of manhood. Let God teach him how to be who and what you need.

I know that some of the strongest, most intelligent and successful men want a warm, concerned shoulder to lean on. However, if you cross the line from concern to mothering, eventually he will feel smothered. Soon after that, you will talk more to his voice mail than to him. He will run for cover. Men want freedom, like comfort and desire support. They are most at ease without pressure. The crazy thing is that once he gets bored with you, he finds another mother and you are left bitter, angry and feeling used. A strong and confident man wants a partner not a parent.

If you need to mother something get a puppy, a kitten or a goldfish. Better yet, find a local organization that allows you to be a mentor or big sister to a child who will flourish as you impart of your wonderfulness.

Life Lessons Learned In This Chapter

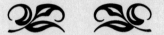

LOVE LEAVES ROOM FOR GROWTH
AND POSITIVE CHANGE

- The key to positive relationships is balance.
- Get out of the way of consequences so growth can take place.
- Your partner is not your child—he is your partner.
- Men don't want to be smothered—they want to be supported.
- Men don't want to be mothered—they want to be encouraged.

Scripture

Wisdom is the principal thing; therefore get wisdom.
And in all your getting, get understanding.

Proverbs 4:7

Written Affirmation

Share Your Thoughts

I will not over-nurture my relationships because:

_____

_____

_____

_____

_____

_____

_____

Melissa's Story

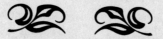

ALWAYS THE VICTIM
(It's Not My Fault)

*M*elissa was about to get written up again. She is on her fourth job in nine months because she is always late and she always has an excuse. Either her alarm didn't go off or the traffic was bad or she wasn't feeling well. The amazing thing about Melissa is that it's never her fault. When her supervisor asked her for the monthly report due on the twenty-fifth, Melissa said it wasn't ready because the computer was down for a couple of hours. Further, the other departments had not submitted their reports on time so that she could compile the information and have it ready for the monthly senior staff meeting.

This behavior wasn't reserved just for her job, it spilled over into everything Melissa did. At church she was a member of the Hospitality Ministry. She never volunteered to do anything extra because she didn't want to be responsible in case something went wrong.

More than anything, Melissa constantly resisted change because it required too much of her time to make adjustments to her routine. Her life was cool just the way it was. Her home life wasn't much better. Melissa never, ever paid her bills on time because she didn't feel as though she had to. If her phone got cut off, it was no big deal. She'd just have it turned back on the next time she got paid. The two credit cards Melissa had were of no use to her because they were constantly over the limit. Somehow, Melissa rationalized that shopping made her feel better so she usually spent money she didn't have. Life happens, and when it does, just blame somebody else.

$\mathcal{V}$ictory is always found past your limitations. Frequently, we give up too soon, turn around too fast and quit. Persistence is based on character and character does what is right—not what is easy. Endurance is acquired through steady focus and determination. Success comes from solutions, not excuses, passion, not pity parties, discipline, not perpetual discouragement, answers, not agendas, and from simply making a decision to be the best, no matter what. It takes courage to be who God made you to be and to do what He created you to do.

The difference between winning and losing is attitude and a willingness to take personal responsibility for our thoughts, our choices and ultimately our actions. It's time for you to take responsibility for your actions. You have skated over and skirted around issues long enough. Have you ever wondered why every time you are involved, the same negative situations arrive? It is because you can't get away from you. You are with you everywhere you go.

Sometimes, particularly in cases of domestic violence, women are victims. That's not what I am referring to here. I mean, really, is it always the other person's fault that the relationship did not work or is not working?

You whine, you complain, you cry and you are never satisfied. If things don't go the way you think they should go, look out world, because here comes a train with no conductor that will soon derail and crash. Whenever things must always be a certain way, you will be miserable because life constantly changes and believe it or not, so do you.

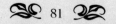

Self-pity is a form of selfishness. It is an enemy of love and hinders our ability to love. It is an exaggeration of self-concern. Love looks through a telescope and self-pity looks through a microscope. Self-pity is also another form of pride. A consuming love of self prohibits your complete surrender to God's will for your life.

The Bible says in Proverbs 16:18, Pride goes before destruction, and a haughty spirit before a fall.

I love you. That's the reason I wrote this book. Since no one else will tell you—I will. Get yourself together so you can move on. Some pieces of your experience may not be salvageable. However, take what's left and live. Haven't you been miserable long enough? How long are you going to sit there and complain about what's not being done for you? In Christ, there is always a way. Get up and do it yourself.

Is that it? You don't want to do anything so that if it goes wrong you can't be blamed? Are you too scared and weak to come out of your shell and enjoy life? People who are always the victim are afraid to fail. It's time for you to move to higher ground. Here's an excerpt from one of my messages that I hope provokes you to change.

We are in a season where God is raising up a remnant that is not afraid. God is recruiting those who will not allow religious expectations to keep you lame. God has the Body of Christ in a place where we expect the unusual and we no longer have to sit around saved and crippled. No longer do we have to be in church and still not know God. No longer do we have to be intimidated by what we perceive to be the anointing but is really a form of godliness. In this season, you shall know the truth and the truth that you apply to your life will make you free. Truth is what God says—religion is what man says God says. If you are really in pursuit of life in the High Places, then you need an encounter with God. ✳

✳When you really want God, you'll do whatever it takes. You won't try and bend God to your agenda. You'll become pliable to what He wants for you. You'll begin to recognize, understand and know that what's coming is better than what's been. ✳

✳When you let go of something, it's because you know you're about to reach for something else. God is challenging you to risk having nothing for a moment so that you can have it all. You're in a critical and pivotal place of never again and never before. Never again will you go through that and never before (if you respond appropriately) have you seen what God is about to do. This place is called *transition*. Transition has been hired by God to drive you from where you are to where God has called you to be. Transition teaches you who you are, transition makes you grow and transition polishes you for the promise. However, quite frequently, we resist transition because transition requires transformation. ✳

Where you are right now is not all there is—even when it's your fault. The upheaval in your life right now is the rearranging, reordering, renewing, refreshing, restoring, renovating, regenerating hand of God that comes to shift you from where you are to where you need to be. When God speaks a word, your faith is *only* activated by your movement. Which means when God speaks, you must do something. Said another way, when God moves, you must move—just like that.

God wants us to get over our silent contentions, frustrations, fears and weaknesses. In order to do this effectively, we must embrace the revelation of who we are as believers to unlock our "potent authority" as kings and priests in the earth. Until you get this understanding, you'll be so consumed by your future or so oppressed by your past that you'll mismanage your now.

There is always something beyond where you are. You must stop rehearsing the past! What are you holding on to that God has asked you to let go of? You must start pressing toward the promise. The promise is Jesus. In Him we live, move and have our being. In Him we have fullness of joy. You must stay focused using praise as a stabilizer—being steadfast, immovable, always abounding in the work of the Lord. Today is the first day of the best days of your life. Living in the High Places of God means:

Exposure: Revelation of who God is in you and who you are in Him.

Expansion: Increase and harvest in every area of your life.

Experience: Maturity and authority in your walk with Him.

In this next move of God in the earth, God is manifesting impossibilities and releasing increased capacity to people who never thought they could have it. God is in-

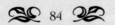

creasing your integrity, your peace, your joy, your love, your patience, your compassion, your contentment and your worship.

God is ready to shift you into position because what you have right now is not all that God has for you. What God has for you is in the next dimension—the High Places. In order to embrace this place you must do three things:

1. Leave alone stuff and people that are not working

We get frustrated where we are because we exhaust our capacity in that place and stay too long. Too often, we would rather struggle with something than be whole with nothing. In order to walk and live in the High Places of God you must deal with "that thing" or "those people" and destroy the connection or the connection will destroy you.

2. Live a life of absolute obedience

Isaiah 1:19 declares that if you are willing and obedient then you shall eat of the plenty of the land. The demand of God in your life unlocks His power in your life. It's time for us to get back to holiness. It is possible to live a life of obedience. Our battle is not with the devil. Our battle is between our standards and our options. Our struggle is between what God says about us and what we think about ourselves. You must move from where you are because being stuck is no longer conducive to what God wants to do in your life. *Obedience releases opportunity and opportunity produces overflow.*

3. Long for His presence

Long for His presence the way you long for your favorite thing or person. I remember several years ago being so connected to a person that I was devastated when, in his words, he loved me enough to leave me alone because he knew he was not in a place to be what or who I needed. I cried for days. I vividly remember driving to work one morning during this period with tears streaming down my face. God said to me, "Dry your tears and listen to me. I know your heart is aching. I know you feel as though your core has been ripped out. Vikki, I know you love him. However, I want you to want me like that! I want you to want to be around me like that! I want you to desire my presence in your world like that."

Later that same week, a close friend confirmed what I had heard the Lord say to me. Basically, my friend said, "God has your ear, but He wants your whole heart." Needless to say, my emotional whirlwind came to an abrupt end and I began to realize the power of His presence in my life.

In His presence there is fullness of joy. In the overflow is where God pours the oil of joy into the dry places in your life. In the overflow is where miracles overwhelm you. There is a place in God where I no longer deal with defeat. All things work together for my good and for perpetual victory in my life. There is a place in God where I rise above every circumstance and come out victorious. God wants us to come up to a higher plane to commune with Him.

In the High Places of God is where strange voices are quieted. In the High Places God releases wealth untold. In the High Places you hear what is in heaven before it is released on earth.

The vehicle to life in the High Places is prophetic praise. Praise is always appropriate. Praise releases power. Praise releases purity. Praise releases passion. Praise releases purpose and ushers you into the High Places. Psalm 37:5 commands us to commit our way to the Lord, trust in Him and He shall bring it to pass. Your praise becomes prophetic once you commit to obedience and trust God no matter what.

If you are ready to move, then you must become a person of praise. Praise will change your life forever. Yes, wherever you are reading this, prepare your atmosphere with praise and worship. If you know you were born to do the ridiculous, then praise. If you know God has greater for you and you are ready to be cast into the un-believable, then praise. If you are ready to see what God sees, hear what God hears, love what God loves, and hate what He hates, then you must praise God even when you do not understand what He is doing in your life.

If you are ready for your pain to become power, your misery to become ministry, your worry to become worship, your trauma to become triumph, your weakness to become a Kingdom weapon, then you must become a prophetic praiser. When you come out of this you will not be the same, because in an atmosphere of praise, con-version takes place. As you allow God to establish you in the High Places, His promise to you is found in Deuteronomy 28:1-13:

1   If you will listen diligently to the voice of the Lord your God, being watchful to do all His com-mandments which I command you this day, the Lord your God will set you high above all the na-tions of the earth.

2   And all these blessings shall come upon you and overtake you if you heed the voice of the Lord your God.

3   Blessed shall you be in the city and blessed shall you be in the field.

4   Blessed shall be the fruit of your body and the fruit of your ground and the fruit of your beasts, the increase of your cattle and the young of your flock.

5   Blessed shall be your basket and your kneading trough.

6   Blessed shall you be when you come in and blessed shall you be when you go out.

7   The Lord shall cause your enemies who rise up against you to be defeated before your face; they shall come out against you one way and flee before you seven ways.

8   The Lord shall command the blessing upon you in your storehouse and in all that you undertake. And He will bless you in the land which the Lord your God gives you.

9   The Lord will establish you as a people holy to Himself, as He has sworn to you, if you keep the commandments of the Lord your God and walk in His ways.

10 And all people of the earth shall see that you are called by the name of the Lord, and they shall be afraid of you.

11 And the Lord shall make you have a surplus of prosperity, through the fruit of your body, of your livestock, and of your ground, in the land which the Lord swore to your fathers to give you.

12 The Lord shall open to you His good treasury, the

heavens, to give the rain of your land in its season and to bless all the work of your hands; and you shall lend to many nations, but you shall not borrow.

13 And the Lord shall make you the head, and not the tail; and you shall be above only, and you shall not be beneath, if you heed the commandments of the Lord your God which I command you this day and are watchful to do them.

The good news is that failure is just success turned inside out. Want more good news? You can do all things through Christ Jesus who strengthens you.

Life Lessons Learned In This Chapter

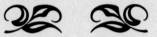

<u>LOVE IS RESPONSIBLE FOR WHAT LOVE REQUIRES</u>

- Character does what is right — not what is easy.
- Endurance is acquired through steady focus and determination.
- Success comes from solutions not excuses.
- It takes courage to be all that God made you to be and to do what He created you to do.

Scripture

Wait on the Lord, be of good courage, and He shall strengthen your heart; Wait, I say on the Lord.

Psalm 27:14

Written Affirmation

Share Your Thoughts

I will not play the victim and I will take responsibility for my actions because:

_____

_____

_____

_____

_____

_____

_____

_____

Valerie's Story

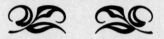

BEING THE SPARE TIRE
(The Other Woman)

"*I never meant for this to happen*," Valerie told her counselor. "*It didn't start out this way. It was innocent and I simply enjoyed talking to Kevin. That's all it was. After sharing so much of my story with him during our new members' conference, it just became easy to talk to him when I needed someone to listen. Most of the time he asked me to call him at the church because it was easier to reach him there. Then he started calling me at my office and then at my house just to say hi. I was flattered that my pastor thought I was attractive and intelligent and witty. After all, I had only been attending the church for a few months. I felt special that he noticed me out of 2,500 people. It made me feel good that although Lady Ramsey was exquisitely beautiful and anointed in her own right, Pastor Ramsey made time after hours to check on me.*

"One day I was home because I wasn't feeling well. Kevin called and asked if I needed him to bring me anything. Initially I told him that I was all right and just needed to rest. He insisted that I allow him to stop by just for a few moments because he had something he wanted to share with me. I thought nothing of it. About an hour later my doorbell rang and it was my handsome pastor Kevin Ramsey. For some reason, he took my breath away as he stood there in a mock turtleneck and pair of jeans. I hadn't really paid much attention to his physique before—but 'Help me Lord, this man is fine.'

"He said that he was thinking about me and really wanted to see me. I turned around and walked away from the door to let him in. As I turned back around he was right behind me and kissed me on the lips in a way that I had never been kissed before. I'm not going to lie—I kissed him back. There was no more talking after that. My clothes came off and so did his. We had a couple of hours of the most passionate sex ever. From that point on, our affair lasted eighteen months. We hooked up at my house every Wednesday afternoon, which was easy. I had a successful real-estate business so I managed my own schedule. It all came crashing down after I found out I was pregnant with twins. I never told him. I just quietly packed my things, tied up some loose ends, changed my numbers and relocated here to Houston. I now live in one of my investment properties with my beautiful six-month-old, identical twin girls. Deep down inside, the guilt is eating away at me. Maybe one day I'll tell him about his girls. Then again, maybe not."

The right thing at the wrong time is still the wrong thing. Affairs are probably the most prevalent form of counterfeit love today. People indulge in this behavior for many reasons. Some of these reasons include physical attraction, the excitement of risk, curiosity, the desire to escape or find relief from a painful relationship, boredom, a desire to fill gaps in an existing union, a desire to punish one's partner, the need to prove one's attractiveness or worth and the desire for attention. However, crumbs are not worth waiting for!

Affairs are glamorized in movies, soap operas, in music lyrics, prime-time television shows, and we as a culture are enamored and fascinated by the details of such occurrences. Sex is not reserved for late-night cable television anymore. The reality of the times we live in is that sex sells. It sells movie tickets, vacations, air fresheners and, if you look in the average magazine on any rack, sex sells food, liquor and even medicine. Further, there is a lack of effective sex education, first in the home, then at school, then at church, at work and in our culture — period. The access to sexual content without appropriate education is equivalent to allowing a five-year-old to play with a loaded gun. It's a dangerous and life-threatening thing — literally. The existence of shame and discomfort surrounding sex makes it difficult for partners to talk honestly about sex.

We tend to think that only bad people have affairs or become the other woman (or the other man). That is not true. Most people don't intend to have an affair and most people don't think it will happen to them, but it does.

Interestingly, a lot of women state that they prefer to

be the other woman. They don't care about the commitment because they have their freedom and independence. However, when the holidays and special days come around, their reality hits quite hard. Emotions such as sadness, loneliness and isolation somehow seem to take over.

Okay—let's say you're the other woman. Let me ask you this—did you just spend another special day alone? Or maybe he was able to stop by for fifteen minutes while his wife thinks he is running errands. Perhaps he lives in another city, which makes the longing worse because you are left with rental movies, popcorn and glancing at the phone, hoping he will at least call. When are you going to realize that you are just his dirty little secret? Do not fool yourself into believing you serve any other purpose than to satisfy his insatiable sexual appetite.

If others know, it's only a few people—and I assure you, they have shared your secret with their best friend. Did you know every one has another best friend?

If you are the other woman, you are not as important as you think you are to him. He does not care about your promotion, your child's Christmas program at school, or even how your day went. His only concern, in spite of what he says, is when is the next time you want to have sex. Take a moment and examine your time together. I am willing to bet that he is always available in the good times, not the hard times. Every woman who is the other woman thinks that her situation is unique. It's unique only because *you* are unique. However, at the core of every extramarital affair are the same elements, the same excuses, the same reasoning, the same lies, the same unrealistic expectations and the same disappointment.

Men who are involved with two women at the same time are selfish. It is totally about them. The sex is good because the situation is wrong on so many levels. No matter how you rationalize the details, you are second. It is easy for him to convince you that you are doing all the things his "main woman" will not do, but that's because you are not living a normal life together. The two of you experience stolen moments.

I feel your pain and understand your misery. The thing is, this is never going to be different. The drudgery of being the spare tire or the other woman never changes. He is never around when it really counts. He is with his wife and children. You are left to daydream about a day that will *never* come. What day is that? I'm glad you asked. It's the day he divorces his wife and marries you. I know you are reading this and saying that I don't understand, that your relationship is different. He really loves you.

Further, you personally know of a woman who was the mistress and became the wife. Guess what? I know of those cases too and they are the exception, not the rule. Further still, if he does leave his wife and marry you, you will live with the eternal fear of payback, because what goes around does come back around—eventually. You will also live with the ever-present insecurity of wondering if he is doing to you what you helped him to do to his ex-wife.

The excitement of your "lust affair" is the fact that there is no real commitment or covenant. At the end of the day, you provide an intense and passionate physical release as well as an emotional and temporary escape from his reality. Are you angry yet? You should be, and I hope you are angry enough to realize that you deserve better. You deserve to be a man's priority, not one of his options. You deserve to be the only object of one man's affection, adoration and attention.

When he talks about you to his boys, are you his freak or his first lady? Are you his piece or his true passion? Are you just a distraction for him or his heart's desire?

You deserve to be with him in the light as well as in the dark. You deserve to be introduced to his family, his friends, his pastor and his children if he has them. Whenever you settle for less than God intended, it is always mediocre and never fully satisfying. When God is pleased with your choice there is no lack anywhere.

A dear friend of mine once told me that something can be valued without being valid. This statement of truth negates the pleasure and long-term joy of having someone special in your life. It's like living the ultimate dream that turns into a nightmare because the high you experience is temporary.

Good sex in bad (unhealthy) relationships is intoxicating.

Passion literally means suffering and it is often the case that the greater the suffering, the deeper the passion. The Greeks distinguished what we call love as *eros* (passionate love) and *agape* (stable and committed love, free of passion). It follows then, that *eros* is the feeling of suffering for love and *agape* is the feeling of love in a stable and committed environment free of suffering.

Eros, in this context, is defined as an all-consuming, desperate yearning for the beloved, who is perceived as different, mysterious and elusive. The depth of love is measured by the intensity of the obsession. There is little time or attention for other interests or pursuits, because so much energy is focused on past encounters or on imagining future ones.

Agape describes a deep caring and concern between two people who share many basic values, interests and goals, and who tolerate good-naturedly their individual differences. The depth of this connection is measured by the mutual trust and respect they feel toward each other.

When you are the spare tire, the price you pay for passion is fear. The very pain and fear that feed your passionate encounters with your love also eventually destroy it.

How can you begin to get out of this arrangement? First, change your mind about being the other woman for the rest of your life. If he will not make immediate changes in your favor, then get out. Second, only make ultimatums that you intend to carry out. Third, find someone you trust to confide in as a point of accountability.

For goodness sakes, don't get pregnant in an attempt to trap him. Trapping him is trapping yourself, and it is a horrible beginning for the innocent child. Find things and people that interest you apart from him. The better you feel about yourself, the quicker you will separate yourself from the things that cause you to compromise.

There is someone who wants you and you only. Honesty with yourself is the key to your wholeness. Open and honest communication is also essential to effective recovery. Affairs are about anything but love; they are usually the coming together of one emotionally vulnerable adult and another adult seeking sexual gratification. This is not a healthy, loving relationship. This is not the solution to what led you to an affair in the first place. You deserve the best and God absolutely wants you to have it.

Life Lessons Learned In This Chapter

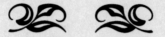

<u>LOVE DOESN'T ASK YOU TO COMPROMISE YOUR VALUES</u>

- We tend to think only bad people have affairs.
- Most people don't intend to have an affair.
- Men involved with two women at the same time are selfish.
- If you are the "other woman" you will always be second.
- The right thing at the wrong time is still the wrong thing.
- There is someone who wants you and *only* you.

Scripture

But as for me, I will walk in my integrity; redeem me and be merciful to me.

Psalms 26:11

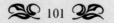

Written Affirmation

Share Your Thoughts

I will not settle for being the other woman because:

_____

_____

_____

_____

_____

_____

_____

Maria's Story

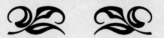

I'LL DO WHATEVER YOU WANT
(People-pleasing)

Maria *was one of the most talented event planners I had ever met. She could plan a wedding, a birthday party, an anniversary celebration, an engagement dinner or a bridal shower. It didn't matter. The girl had skills. People noticed her skills and often asked her to help them coordinate some upcoming festivity. Maria did help, and the thing that made me angry about my roommate is that she didn't get paid. She did all this stuff for free while working as a medical assistant.*

Our next-door neighbor Andrew noticed Maria too…but not for her talent alone. He thought she was attractive and was drawn to her "little girl innocence," as he called it. Andrew wanted to marry Maria, and she knew it. However, Andrew found it quite difficult to spend quality time with Maria because she was always agreeing to help someone with time she really didn't have. "Why do you work so hard, Maria?" Andrew asked her often. Her response was that she really wanted people to accept and like her.

All her life she had been an outcast and had had to perform for people to be pleased with her. The only way Maria knew to get love and attention was to do something to earn it. In Maria's homeland of Mexico, that's what women did. They did whatever they had to do to get done whatever they needed to get done.

Maria told Andrew about the countless times she'd had to dance for her brothers and their friends to avoid being brutally punished by her father. Maria told Andrew how when she turned seventeen, she decided to take a chance and cross the border alone in the middle of the night hoping to find a better way of living. Now that she is here in the United States, it seems to be so hard for Maria to let go of old patterns of behavior. Maria eventually began to recognize that people will use you until they use you up.

I finally convinced Maria to go to school so that she could finally start her business as an event planner. It's going to take some time to break old habits. The good news is that she is trying and Andrew is still waiting.

People-pleasing is a miserable way to live. Just when you think "they" are satisfied, they change their minds. Breaking the cycle of approval takes great courage. Are you one of those people who feels guilty when you say no? This word seems to escape the vocabulary of a lot of women. Perhaps it is because you grew up thinking the only way to feel love is to perform for it. Maybe you gather pieces of self-worth—notice I said *pieces*—from making life better for everyone else. So you say yes even when you want to say no, only to resent the choice, resent the people you decided to help and resent yourself. Overloaded people fail. This pattern of behavior is particularly destructive not just in romantic relationships, but on the job, in the family and with friends.

It is not realistic to take the position, "I am happy only if I can make someone else happy." When that is your measurement of self-worth, it is a sign that you are a fractured or broken person. This behavior is due more to conditioning than to character flaw. Most people who embrace this attitude learned or observed this method as the way to get and keep a man.

The insane thing is that you continue this pattern of behavior knowing in advance the outcome is only going to add more frustration and anxiety to your already chaotic existence. This cycle is usually connected to feelings of guilt. Guilt renders our coping skills useless to a point. It also strengthens our need to attempt to lessen the guilt by doing things for people that we don't want to be bothered with. The end result—more guilt and resentment.

Remember the movie *Coming to America* and the scene

of the arranged wedding? The prince, played by Eddie Murphy, was being introduced for the first time to his soon-to-be bride, played by Vanessa Bell Calloway. The prince was very uncomfortable with the arranged marriage and wanted a few moments to get to know this beautiful woman. They went into a side room for privacy so that he could ask her a few questions. He asked her, "What do you like to eat?" She replied, "Whatever you like to eat." He asked her, "What type of music do you like?" She replied, "Whatever type of music you like." He then told her to hop on one foot and bark like a dog. She did it and he immediately rushed out of the room and out of the palace to pack his bags and depart for America. Most men want a strong woman beside them.

This behavior can be corrected when we accept the truth that no one can make you feel guilty, inferior or worthless without your agreement. The moment you understand that your self-worth comes from God and that you don't have to perform for love—you are free. The moment you embrace that you are accepted in the beloved family of God by God—even if it means some people won't like your new identity—you are free.

Meeting relational needs and being a pleaser are two very different things. The difference is that relational needs are met because the person is the incentive. Living to be a pleaser has less to do with the person than with constantly performing for the person, with or without their permission or enjoyment.

It's time for you to begin investing time in priorities that bring you a high return. I'll let you in on a little secret found in a book a lot of people don't take the time to read.

It says, and I am paraphrasing, when you find out what pleases the Lord, He will then begin to give you the desires of your heart.

People-pleasing yields consistently low returns. God-pleasing produces blessings you will not have room enough to receive. What others say, think or feel about you isn't nearly as important as what you say to yourself after they have stopped talking. It may be uncomfortable at first. However, short-term discomfort is better than spending the rest of your life feeling like a bird in a cage.

Life Lessons Learned In This Chapter

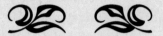

<u>LOVE SAYS NO SOMETIMES</u>

- People-pleasing is a miserable way to live.
- Breaking this cycle of approval takes great courage.
- No one can make you feel guilty, inadequate or worthless without your agreement.
- People-pleasing consistently yields low returns on the investment of time.
- You must understand that your self-worth comes from God.

Scripture

For do I now persuade men or God? Or do I seek to please men? For if I still pleased men, I would not be a bondservant of Christ.

Galatians 1:10

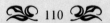

Written Affirmation

Share Your Thoughts

I will live to be celebrated and not tolerated because:

_____

_____

_____

_____

_____

_____

_____

Patrice's Story

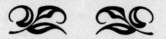

IT'S NOT WHAT YOU THINK
(Denial)

The documentary had just ended and Patrice sat stunned. She couldn't move. Could it be true? Could it be that what she suspected had just been proven? The hour-long program had talked about the devastating consequences when men are having sex with both men and women. It talked about how Black women are the largest group of newly infected HIV cases because their men are living on the "down low."

Manny is too masculine to be gay, she thought. We have a wonderful marriage of ten years, a wonderful love life and our kids are happy. He takes care of us and to my knowledge he has never lied to me. Then again, I never ask him any questions either. I remember finding his little brown book in his trunk in the basement behind the stack of boxes, with the names of men, dates and their phone numbers. I just assumed they were business associates or friends we never talked about. Now that I reflect on that day, he had red stars by some of them and two red stars by others. This is not happening to me!

What about the time you came home and he was lounging

around with just his shorts on. All of a sudden, Bobby came out of the back room with just his shorts on and they told you that they had just finished working out. Could it be that it wasn't the kind of working out I assumed? The house didn't smell like sweat. As a matter of fact, it smelled like a candle that had obviously been burning for a couple hours. Nah—couldn't be.

Stop thinking like that, Patrice. Manny would not do that to you. He loves you too much.

What about the time your sister called you and told you she thought she saw Manny down under the bridge near the gay club and you cursed her out? You didn't speak to your sister for months. Could she have been right? Absolutely not—Manny loves women too much to be having sex with men. I know how to please my husband. Lord, what should I do? Should I go get one of those HIV tests they talked about on the show? What should I do? Never mind, Lord. If I am sick like those women they talked to on that program—I'd really rather not know. I'd really rather not know.

Suddenly her husband walked through the door and Patrice went into her usual routine. "Oh, welcome home, honey. How was your day? Dinner will be ready in a few minutes." She silently vowed not to ask any questions that would upset the quiet life they shared.

This chapter is short, sweet and straight to the point. You cannot change what you will not acknowledge! Too many women live in denial, accepting substandard treatment due to fear of being alone.

Once when I was adjudicating a situation, my friend and colleague Jean Rozier asked me, "Vikki, don't you see that elephant in the living room?" I laughed so hard I had tears streaming down my face. After a while, however, I thought about the point she made. How can you *not* see what is wrong? It is so obvious that it is hard, almost impossible, to miss.

Frequently, the answer is that we do not want to see it or we do not want to know it. Deception, even self-deception, lies in the heart of those who think reality has nothing to offer.

Do you remember the time your girlfriend told you she saw your man out on the town with someone that wasn't you? You never addressed or researched the information she gave you. You got angry with your friend for having the audacity to tell you what she saw — not with him. How crazy is that? The mind is a powerful thing. Or maybe your problem is that you have found evidence that proves deception is taking place and yet you still act as if nothing is wrong.

Denial is a powerful defense mechanism that can be defined, according to author Robin Norwood, a licensed marriage, family and child therapist, as a refusal to acknowledge reality on two levels: First, at the level of what is actually happening, and second, at the level of feeling. She further states, "Denial feeds the need to control, and

the inevitable failure to control feeds the need to deny."
The Bible tells us in the book of John that you shall know
the truth, and I would emphasize that only the truth you
apply to your life will make you free.

Life Lessons Learned In This Chapter

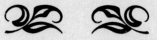

LOVE EMBRACES TRUTH

- You cannot change what you will not acknowledge.
- Reality has more to offer you than living in denial.
- Denial is a defense mechanism.
- Truth you know and then apply is the only way to freedom.

Scripture

For we can do nothing against the truth, but for the truth.

2 Corinthians 13:8

Written Affirmation

Share Your Thoughts

I will seek to live in truth, to tell the truth and to promote truth because:

_____

_____

_____

_____

_____

_____

_____

Tiffany's Story

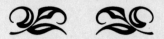

I DON'T HAVE ROOM FOR A MAN IN MY LIFE
(Independence)

Tiffany Sweeting was living the life of her dreams in Charlotte, NC. She had recently received her MBA/JD from the University of North Carolina at Chapel Hill and had been selected to work for one of the most prestigious business development firms in the southeast United States. She was making well over six figures, on her way to seven, had recently put the finishing touches on her brand-new home, and was driving a customized, convertible Jaguar. Single, no children, and in her early thirties this woman had it made. She could have any guy she wanted. She had season's tickets to the Carolina Panthers and to the Charlotte Hornets. She was what we call a "pretty Black girl" down here in the South. She was smart too. Her dark complexion was flawless. Her ebony eyes were accentuated with naturally long eyelashes, perfectly arched eyebrows, and that short haircut always looked like she had just left the salon.

The older people at the Right Way Missionary Baptist Church really liked Tiffany. She volunteered to work with the

Meals On Wheels program. She helped prepare and deliver food to the sick and shut-in every Tuesday. One particular afternoon, Sister Mabel Henry asked Tiffany when she was gonna settle down and start a family. Tiffany laughed it off and kept working. "No time soon, Mother Henry, no time soon." Mother Henry asked Tiffany the same question every week. After about the thirty-fifth time, Tiffany asked Mother Henry, "Why is that answer so important to you?" Mother Henry said, "Child, I've been waiting for you to ask me that. I see ya round here with your fancy car, fancy clothes and pretty smile. I just noticed over the last few months, every time one of these nice young men approaches you and tries to talk, you seem to wave them off like they are flies or something. Girl, I am seventy-six years young and going strong. I used to be you. I've never been married, never had any children, and now that I'm preparing to leave all my money to my nieces, nephews, the Black college down the road, and some to the church, I don't want you to end up like me—alone with all my stuff. I remember when you were a baby round here. Now that your parents are deceased and you pretty much don't have any family, somebody needed to step to you with this wisdom. You remind me so much of myself when I was your age. After I say this I won't ask you no more 'bout when you gone settle down. If you are honestly happy, then good. If you are staying away from love because you are afraid of getting hurt—then that is not so good. Success means nothing at the end of the day unless you have somebody to share it."

We all know her. She is successful, brilliant, attractive, confident and physically fit. She loves sports, theater, fine dining, takes exotic vacations, and has not one, but two luxury automobiles. She is civic-minded, socially conscious and politically astute. She's known as a "man-magnet" because she always seems to be in the company of one successful, handsome man or another.

This chapter is not to challenge you if you are authentically happy. However, it is to provoke you to examine whether you are living a life of outward success and inward turmoil. Are you really living life with passion and purpose? Or are you stressed out, trying to maintain the accumulated liabilities that reflect how many years you went to school and how many sixty-hour weeks you have worked in corporate America making someone else wealthy? Are you enjoying the fruits of your labor or just enduring the work week to rest on the weekends to start over again on Monday? Are you living your dreams, or are you killing yourself to prove to your parents, siblings, childhood friends and teachers that you are important and smart?

Sometimes, overachievers re-create the very scenario they worked so hard to avoid. In the interim, the over-achiever secretly and quietly longs for significance in some one else's life. These women destroy their relationships by being too controlling, too bossy and too demanding, which turns men off. Deep down inside, the truth is that the woman is insecure and fears rejection so she rejects him first.

The scenario can look like this: You meet a guy you

really like—you are truly attracted to him. However, since you are accustomed to being in charge, you only let him in so far because you will not be made to look silly or stupid. Let the games begin.

You are feeling secure because playing games is what you do well. You are a competitor and you have studied enough to know that the game is the same—only the players change. You move. He moves. You study his responses and move again. He comes closer and you back away a little. Now the stakes are raised because it is going just the way you planned—you are in control again—and he is playing right into your hands.

Just when you think you've got him in a space that fits your world, he moves again—but this time out the door. You start playing the game again and keep playing until you meet another guy who will acquiesce to your charm. For real, sis, while you are being "in charge" and keeping your heart in a padlocked box, your reality is that nothing significant comes in and nothing significant goes out. At the end of the day, all you have is your degrees, your nice things, your accomplishments, your family that is tremendously proud of you, your wonderful home and *nobody to share it with*.

Is that really how you want to live? I could easily be you. As a matter of fact, I *was* you. Then I had an encounter with God and allowed Him to soften my heart toward Him, rebuild my trust in Him and increase my capacity to be vulnerable. Once you seek the Lord, everything else will be added (including the right man for you) if that is what you desire.

We have all been hurt in love. I played sports in school

and am still very active. One thing that was consistent among my coaches, no matter the sport and no matter the team, was the statement "no pain, no gain." I was conditioned to endure discomfort for the sake of ultimate victory and success. It's the same with love. Each new experience offers something valuable and prepares us for the next encounter—even if it does not work out the way it was originally planned.

Stop treating your relationships with men as though they are business deals. Be open, be witty, and when you least expect it, God will manifest a bonus in your life!

Life Lessons Learned In This Chapter

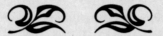

LOVE HELPS YOU BALANCE ALL THAT LIFE HAS FOR YOU

- When you live life devoid of interdependent relationships, you miss so much.
- The lack of trust in God will lead you to live a life of mistrust when it comes to others.
- Allow God to soften your heart toward Him and He will soften your heart toward others.
- No pain, no gain—the road map to ultimate victory.

Scripture

For I know the thoughts that I think toward you, says the Lord, thoughts of peace and not of evil, to give you a future and a hope.

Jeremiah 29:11

Written Affirmation

Share Your Thoughts

I will live my life totally trusting God to put all of the pieces of the puzzle together because:

Bethany's Story

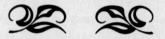

HE DIDN'T MEAN IT
(Abuse)

Bethany and Calvin met while they were both liberal arts majors at a prestigious university. During their freshman orientation they ended up in the same tour group because they were both student athletes. Bethany was attending college on a volleyball scholarship, and Calvin was the well-publicized, hotly recruited incoming quarterback. They hit it off immediately. Bethany took it lightly when Calvin grabbed her arm and yanked her toward him that day. She thought it was cute that after they officially started dating, he wanted to know every detail of her day (who she was with, what she did, where she went, what time she got home, etc.). While her roommates were bothered by Calvin's obsessive behavior, Bethany thought it was adorable. Every now and then, Calvin lost control of his temper and threatened to punch Bethany in the face if she repeated a behavior he didn't like. She never told anyone about those episodes because Calvin could do no wrong in the eyes of the students, staff, alumni or his friends. He's just under a lot of pressure, she thought.

Calvin and Bethany were the sweetheart couple of the campus all four years. Shortly after graduation, just prior to Calvin being drafted by the NFL, they had a storybook wedding and a nightmare honeymoon. As soon as they got into the bridal suite, Calvin backhanded Bethany and told her he didn't appreciate her kissing his friends on their cheeks during the receiving line at the wedding reception. Bethany was so shocked she couldn't move. Immediately Calvin grabbed her, apologized, started kissing her over the imprint of his hand on her face, and then said that he hated that she makes him react like that, but he couldn't help himself. That night, as he was making love to her, she was staring at the ceiling, feeling pangs of regret for the prison she now felt trapped in.

Years passed and their dream life turned into Bethany's nightmare. Although Calvin was now the darling of a pro football team and they had a beautiful, waterfront mansion, it felt more like a waterfront prison. The beatings intensified the more successful Calvin became. Bethany rarely saw her family and friends anymore. If she left the house, she was accompanied either by Calvin or by the private security guard Calvin had hired to "protect" his investments (which included his wife). The worst beating so far was last year when Calvin kicked Bethany in the stomach and she miscarried their first child. There was no one to tell about the miscarriage because she had told no one she was pregnant. Unfortunately, she had no friends and her family thought she wanted to be left alone. She rarely returned their calls because Calvin had recording devices on every mode of communication in and around the house. Calvin had strategically isolated her from the people closest to her. Calvin told the people at the emergency room that she had slipped down the stairs in the house. The nurse looked at her and somehow Bethany knew that she knew it wasn't true. The doctor asked Calvin to step into the hallway to go over Bethan's discharge instructions and to get his autograph for his son. In the meantime, the nurse helped her get dressed, gently put her hand over a few old bruises and, without saying a word, discreetly handed her a domestic violence hotline number. She whispered, "When you're ready, they will help you." Bethany never got a chance to use that number. The next week, as she was packing a getaway suitcase, Calvin came home unexpectedly and lost it. "You're not leaving me. You're never leaving me! When you do leave, it will be over my dead body," he screamed. And with that, he shot himself in the head right in front of her! Now he was out of his misery and in a strange way, so was Bethany.

$\mathcal{D}$omestic violence is a serious, widespread problem in America that affects women of all races, socioeconomic status, education, religions and ages. According to a report compiled by the Family Violence Prevention Fund, nearly one-third of American women report being physically or sexually abused by a husband or boyfriend at some point in their lives. While women are less likely than men to be victims of violent crimes overall, women are five to eight times more likely than men to be victimized by an intimate partner. Abuse is a continuous cycle and many women stay with an abusive partner because they think the relationship will get better. Some women have even gone so far as to get an order of protection against their abusive mate, but then they let their guard down after a few weeks/months/apologies and start a friendship again. But much to their dismay, the same old pattern of abuse eventually resurfaces.

Every nine seconds in the United States a woman is assaulted and beaten. Four million women a year are assaulted by their partners. Domestic violence is the number-one cause of emergency room visits by women. Abusive husbands and lovers harass seventy-four percent of employed battered women at work, either in person or over the telephone, causing twenty percent to lose their jobs.

More disturbing is the fact that as many as 324,000 women each year experience intimate partner violence during their pregnancy. On average, approximately four women are murdered by their husbands or boyfriends in this country every day. Women are most likely to be killed when attempting to leave the abuser. In fact, they are at a seventy-five percent higher risk than those who stay.

You say, "He didn't mean it." I say, "Yes, he did!" You say, "He can't help it." I say, "Yes, he can, and he can get help and you can too."

This type of counterfeit love touches me deeply. I personally know of several women who have lost their lives due to domestic violence. The earliest memory I have of this horrible experience is from high school in the mid 1980s. A young woman was sitting outside her aunt's apartment talking to a male friend. She and her boyfriend had recently broken up, much to his chagrin. It was a hot, summer evening and the boyfriend drove up uninvited, got out of his car, walked over to where his ex-girlfriend and her male friend were sitting, shot his ex-girlfriend in the head, shot her male friend, and then shot himself. All three of them died. I did not really comprehend the gravity of this incident until several years later. I simply thought at that time it was an isolated incident. I was so wrong.

Several years later I was having a casual conversation with a childhood friend and asked her how another childhood friend was doing because I had not seen or talked to her in years. She looked at me with a look that said, "Don't you know?" I asked her what was wrong and she informed me that our friend was shot and killed by her husband who then shot and killed himself.

Not knowing where to turn, many women stay in abusive relationships for years, enduring the pain, fear and horror in silence. Too often, these women have children who witness this violence and quite frequently, the children are victims of physical abuse themselves. I know of another case where the "boyfriend" stabbed and killed his girlfriend, stabbed and killed her three-year-old daughter, and then hid for months before finally being caught, convicted and put in prison. He killed the woman because she wanted to end the relationship.

Unfortunately, ninety-three percent of women who kill their mates had been battered by them. Sixty-seven percent killed their mates to protect themselves and their children at the moment of murder. Believe it or not, prison terms for killing husbands are twice as long as for killing wives.

I remember attending the wedding of this next couple. They looked so happy and so "in love." I remember being a little envious of their bliss and wishing one day to have "that kind of chemistry with my man." A few, short years later, I received word that the husband had died from AIDS. Guess what? A couple years after that, the wife also died from AIDS. It is abuse of the *worst* kind to me— deception. You may hear it referred to as "the down low," or MSM (men having sex with men), but they are not gay, bisexual, etc. My point—this man married this woman knowing his former lifestyle but kept it from her.

I'll say it again. Deception is abuse of the worst kind. Men who knowingly marry women or engage in unprotected sexual intercourse with women and also have sex with men are abusers. I am not demonizing men if this is their choice. I do have my personal opinion. However, that is not the intent of this book. I am advocating that women take control of their health—no, take control of their lives—and be responsible. *Ask questions—lots of questions.* Love yourself enough to *ask questions* before you have sex.

If he can't handle the questions and actually give you answers (with proof) then he is not the one for you.

Am I passionate about the "down low" thing? Absolutely I am, because for the last eight years in the course of my work, I've seen "up close and personal" the devastation. I've heard firsthand the stories of women who let their guard down because they trusted someone else to be honest. I have hugged women whose choice of a healthy future was taken away.

We must talk about the deception of men on the "down low." Why? Men on the "down low" don't use condoms (red flag number 1) and most of them don't have their HIV status proven with a certified stamp on the results slip from the local health department (bright-red flag number 2). To wear a condom, in the minds of these men, is to exhibit personal responsibility which robs them of the thrill of this "down low" behavior.

How can you know? The reality of this deception is that most men on the "down low" are not flamboyant nor do they exhibit effeminate tendencies. The first step is to love yourself—truly love yourself. Secondly, have open and frank discussions about sex with your potential partner before you have sex. Thirdly, pay attention to *everything* — his friends, his patterns, his schedule. I'm not saying be suspicious. I am saying pay attention. Next, have a strong circle of male friendships that you can go to for counsel. It's quite invaluable to have an openly gay male friend who can identify what is not so obvious. As the saying goes— "game recognizes game." Trust your instincts and listen to your inner voice. Get tested for HIV together and often if you are sexually active. If he refuses, then say goodbye.

Your life depends on your ability to walk away. Finally, know that men can spot desperation a mile away. Don't succumb to societal pressure to have a man. Settle yourself and believe that you do not have to play the game to win the prize. *You* are the prize!

I talked about it earlier in this book, however, many women know the truth and refuse to deal with their partner's sexual escapades. Denial is a form of counterfeit love because it is rooted in fear. If your man tells you the truth, then please believe him. You can't change him — only God can do that.

Deception is "spiritual deep sleep" and your senses are dulled to reality. Deception is a distortion of the truth. Women have deceived and been deceived since the beginning of time. Here are several examples of deception from the Bible and the spiritual lessons I have learned from each.

Eve was deceived in Genesis 3:4: "But the serpent said to the woman, you shall not surely die." God had given Eve specific instructions not to eat from a particular tree. She did it anyway because the serpent convinced her there would be no consequences. **LESSON**: We must be careful who we listen to.

Rebekah helped her son deceive his father in Genesis 27:15, 16: "Then Rebekah took her elder son Esau's best clothes which were with her in the house, and put them on Jacob her younger son. And she put the skins of the kids on his hands and on the smooth part of his neck." Rebekah helped her son deceive his father to receive an inheritance that did not belong to him. **LESSON**: We must be careful who we help.

Delilah deceived Samson in Judges 16:5: "And the lords of the Philistines came to her and said to her, Entice him and see in what his great strength lies, and by what means we may overpower him that we may bind him to subdue him. And we will each give you eleven hundred pieces of silver." Delilah was a beautiful woman and Samson was very attracted to her. The Philistines knew that Samson was too strong to overtake, so they hired Delilah to use her feminine pulchritude to get information from Samson that eventually cost him his life. **LESSON:** We must be careful what we will do for money.

Tamar was tricked by her brother and then raped in 2 Samuel 13:6: "So Amnon lay down and pretended to be sick; and when the king came to see him, Amnon said to the king, I pray you, let my sister Tamar come and make me a couple of cakes in my sight, that I may eat from her hand." Tamar loved her brother Amnon very much. However, his heart was full of lust for his sister Tamar. So Amnon pretended to be sick and called for his sister to come and take care of him. When she arrived, he raped her and then put her out of the house as if she were worthless. **LESSON**: We must be careful who we trust.

Most abusers are great pretenders in the beginning. They are charmers and specialize in sweeping women off their feet. They are masterful manipulators. They overdo attention, perfection and, in the beginning, are on their best gentlemanly behavior. Classic characteristics that consistently identify abusers are: He is overly concerned with every detail of your life. He calls as soon as you get home. If you're late (because soon after meeting him he knows your schedule), he calls and calls and calls until you answer, "demanding" to know your whereabouts. He quickly shifts from angry to apologetic. He changes from caustic to caring in seconds. Does this sound like someone you know?

Pay attention to the red flags. Don't dismiss them. Your family and friends have tried to warn you about his controlling ways. Snap out of denial and pay attention. Don't fight your help.

Is he inconsiderate, narcissistic, thoughtless, rude, arrogant, possessive and mean-spirited? If you are in the getting-to-know-you stage—*run!* If you are in a committed relationship with him—*break your silence and ask for help!* If you are now out of an abusive relationship, use your "survivor wisdom" and reach back to help another sister.

A very dear friend of mine was married to an emotional and verbal abuser. To my knowledge, he never hit her, but her pain was still very real. It was nothing to hear him tell her how pitiful she was, how grateful she should be that he wanted her because no one else would, how weak and worthless she was, and he often reminded her that she needed him. It got to a point where I stopped going around with them because I could not stand to hear him talk down to her. I could not bear any longer him being so rude to her and then showing the utmost respect and kindness to total strangers.

You may know women like this who take verbal abuse from their mates without defending themselves. It can surely leave you bewildered because the woman used to be self-sufficient, strong, confident and secure. She submitted to his power over her and started believing the lies and lost the will to defend herself and her self-esteem. Not surprisingly, this can happen even to the most confident woman in corporate America who rules the workplace with an iron hand and self-assurance. But when she goes home, she is a shell of her former self.

What is abuse? Simply put, abuse is the misuse of God's original intent. You are the apple of God's eye. Therefore, His original purpose for woman was to be adored, appreciated, affirmed, accepted and admired. There are many types of abuse—physical, emotional, mental, sexual and financial.

Most women end up duplicating the relationship they had or did not have with their father as a little girl. If women grew up with an abusive father, quite frequently they end up in a toxic relationship with an abuser as an adult. If women grew up with a loving, nurturing father, often they end up in healthy, nurturing relationships with men who understand the value and tenderness of femininity.

When children watch a dysfunctional and abusive relationship develop between their parents, they channel and internalize all the negative emotions. This affects them in a negative way and unfortunately, they usually choose a mate who is abusive and the sad cycle continues.

In her book, *Give It to Her*, Sandra Mizell Chaney talks about how many women are in unhealthy relationships without even realizing their situation. A relationship is more than just an ongoing connection with an intimate partner. Relationships range from supervisors to co-workers to family members to children. If you are abused in one relationship, most likely you are being abused in another. If you constantly allow yourself to be taken advantage of with your partner, it can also roll over into your workplace. Coworkers can heap a disproportionate amount of work on you and you will feel helpless to stand up for yourself. There is such a thing as a workplace bully or bosses who are bullies, and they can sense your hesitation and fear. Constant harassment and put-downs can erode your self-esteem, self-confidence and self-worth, thereby affecting many areas of your life at the same time. Remember, abuse is the misuse of God's original intent. People treat us the way we allow them to treat us. People talk to us the way we allow them to talk to us.

I personally know of women who read this book and found the strength to make "life-saving" decisions. If you have no idea what this terror is like, *Give It to Her* will help you avoid this counterfeit trap of love. You see, Sandra is a survivor of domestic violence and now helps other women as a certified domestic violence counselor get out and get on with their lives.

Domestic violence is a breeding ground for counterfeit love and is about someone trying to control another person's very existence. An abuser's own feelings of inferiority cause him to dominate, control and degrade women. An abuser is controlled by fear and consequently uses this same weapon against some of the women in his life.

He may not punch you, but he tears you down by calling you names and gradually isolating you from family and friends. That's emotional and verbal abuse. A man with a healthy sense of love for you will *not* keep you from your family and friends. As a matter of fact, he will encourage you to nurture those relationships and do his part to assist you. He accuses you of cheating (most of the time *he* is cheating), refuses to help when you need it, blames you for his anger, criticizes everything you do, controls the finances to keep you dependent upon him, and the more you try to please him the more displeased he is.

If anyone's treatment of you does not feel right then it is wrong. You are not confused and you are not crazy. It is what it is and deep inside you know you deserve better because you do. I know you feel you can't live without him. I know you think he will change because he has apologized. I know you are afraid and feel you have no options—but you do. If you need help, you can call the National Domestic Violence Hotline at 800-799-SAFE/7233 twenty-four hours a day, seven days a week. You can also visit www.dccadv.org or www.womenslaw.org.

Life Lessons Learned In This Chapter

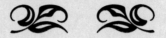

LOVE IS NOT SUPPOSED TO HURT

- ❧ Domestic violence is a serious problem.
- ❧ Every nine seconds a woman is assaulted and beaten.
- ❧ Abuse is the misuse of God's original intent.
- ❧ Deception is abuse of the worst kind.
- ❧ If anyone's treatment of you does not feel right then it is wrong.

Scripture

For God has not given us a spirit of fear, but of power and of love and of a sound mind.

2 Timothy 1:7

Written Affirmation

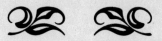

Share Your Thoughts

I will not accept abuse as a form of counterfeit love because:

_____

_____

_____

_____

_____

_____

_____

Dez's Story

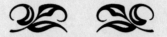

HE IS NOT YOUR DADDY
(Absent Fathers)

Dez met Will over eight years ago when she was just a fourteen-year-old street kid hanging out on the corner. Dez had run away from home because she was tired of being her stepfather's concubine. When Dez told her mother what was going on, her mother spat in her face and called her a lying tramp. Dez's mother spent most of her time in an alcoholic haze and very rarely was lucid enough to be a wife, let alone a mother to Dez and her little brother.

One day after school, Dez dropped her brother off at his father's house and caught the bus a few hours away to start a new life. Dez had made friends with some of Will's "working girls," and they introduced Dez to Will shortly thereafter. Dez learned the tricks of the trade and soon began servicing her own clientele. She liked working for Will. He was her protector and he was like the father she'd never had or ever knew. Will was about forty-two when they met, and he treated Dez a little differently than he treated the other girls. He never hit Dez, never offered her drugs, and he never tried to have sex with Dez because he said she reminded him too much of his own daughter. He thought she was innocent and hated that she was living on the street, but the best he could do was to help her get by from day to day.

Will couldn't afford to get too emotionally involved with Dez. After all, he had a business to run. He did however make a deal with Dez that if she got herself together enough to go to school during the day, she could keep half her money. It was rough, but Dez not only graduated from high school, she graduated from city college too. When Dez heard that Will was killed in a gun fight, she was deeply saddened. She vowed to become all that she could be in his memory and honor. Dez became a very successful vice president at the local bank. However, her personal life was a wreck, especially when it came to her choice in men. She preferred much older men, but most of the time they were either married or involved with someone already. Dez didn't care. She figured that a piece of man was better than no man at all. She reasoned that her days on the street were going to be good for something. Some days are better than others. Some days she sits on her patio and daydreams, wishing that Will was around to see the results of his concern for her. "Will," she says as she looks up to the sky while holding her glass of liquor, "I got some things right and I'm still working on others. I just wish you were here right now to tell me how to get over the fact that my daddy don't even know I exist. It hurts more than you know. I've tried to run away; drink it away; sex it away; drug it away. Will, please tell God that I need his help."

There is not a feeling in the world like being "Daddy's little girl." I'm a Daddy's girl for real. The relationship a girl has with her daddy affects the rest of her life. He's the first impression of a man she had or didn't have. If your daddy was present in your life and poured confidence, approval, stability, security and provision into you, then you have a pretty good foundation when it comes to interacting with men.

Conversely, if your daddy was not around (physically, emotionally, mentally, financially or spiritually), then you may still be searching for him in every relationship you have with a man.

There are many reasons and there are many ways that fathers are absent. Some fathers were never there at all. They simply decided to walk away from the child before the child was born. Other fathers are absent due to death, divorce, drug or alcohol addictions and work. Then there is the father who was in the home physically, but absent emotionally and mentally. The lack of a father's active presence in the life of his daughter can produce years of low self-esteem, low self-worth and low self-confidence.

As little girls, women do not have the emotional and mental capacity to understand the absence of their dad and quite frequently begin searching for this "missing piece" of their lives through unhealthy and often danger-ous ways. One way is to suppress or hide the emotions. Yet another means of coping is to begin a life of compro-mise which leads to unhealthy relationships with men. This is all in an attempt to satisfy a void, an empty hole that cannot be filled. Emotions that accompany this behavior are trepidation, fear of commitment, identity issues, anxiety, depression, anger and lack of intimacy. Many daughters whose fathers were absent grow up to be women who are overachievers, and who overcompensate for any lack in their life by using food, drugs, alcohol and sex. These women also exhibit obsessive-compulsive behaviors that often manifest as neurotic psychotic tendencies that drive men away and damage friendships with other women.

Is your heart on hold? Release it today so that you can begin to heal from the inside out. God wants you to wait on Him for further instructions because He has something wonderful in store for you. God is the ultimate "daddy," and today is the day that you stop looking for what you missed in your relationship with your biological father in your relationships with men. No longer will you medicate the pain from previous relationships by rushing into new ones. The true realization of emotional addiction in relationships is when you recognize not how much you want someone, but how much you fear being without them.

Life Lessons Learned In This Chapter

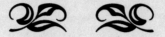

<u>NOBODY CAN LOVE YOU LIKE GOD CAN</u>

- ☙ There is not a feeling in the world like being a daddy's girl.
- ☙ Some women are still "little girls" in their hearts searching for daddy.
- ☙ The lack of a daddy's presence can produce years of esteem issues.
- ☙ Men can't replace your daddy.
- ☙ God is the ultimate daddy.

Scripture

You, O Lord, are the helper of the fatherless.

Psalms 10:14

Written Affirmation

Share Your Thoughts

I will strive to get to know God in a way that makes up for any lack of my daddy's presence in my life because:

_____

_____

_____

_____

_____

_____

_____

Claudia's Story

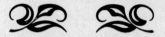

SHE HAS ALL I NEED
(Lesbianism)

*C*andy and Claudia were cheerleaders together in college. Not only that, they were sorority sisters and were both from Los Angeles. They often went to clubs together, dinner together, and were each other's shoulder to cry on when it came to relationship drama. They decided to get an apartment together after graduation as they both got jobs in the city of brotherly love and sisterly affection — Philadelphia. They loved Philly.

Candy was an attorney and Claudia was in her first year of residency at Temple University Hospital. They both worked long hours, hadn't had boyfriends in months and often shared how their love lives had suffered since "real life" began. One evening after a long day at work, Candy came home and fell asleep on the couch in the living room after a long night of fun with some of her co-workers. Candy hadn't gotten much sleep the night before and now it was catching up with her. Claudia came home and chuckled at how wiped out Candy appeared. She didn't bother to wake her. She just threw a blanket on top of Candy and went to her bedroom to go to sleep as she had to be back at the hospital at 5:00 a.m. When Claudia woke up the next morning, she was startled by what sounded like a conversation going on in the living room. It was Candy and her new friend Jesse talking about what had happened between them earlier that week. "Shhhh, Jesse, I don't want to wake Claudia and I certainly don't want her to hear that you and I were making out. It was an accident. I had too much to drink and it won't happen again."

"Candy, who are you fooling? You enjoyed it as much as I did and I am not going to give up on you and me without a fight," Jesse said.

"Give up on us? Jesse, what are you talking about? There is no 'us' and I am not into women like that," Candy said.

"If you say so, Candy Girl, if you say so," Jesse shot back.

What was Claudia hearing? Was Candy bisexual? Was her roommate into women now? "This is not good," she thought to herself as she went into the bathroom to take a shower and get to the hospital. "This can't be good."

This subject historically has been taboo. Homosexuality in general has come to the forefront of our culture, communities, social circles and even our families. This lifestyle is accepted on television and in pop culture. However, many are still uncomfortable discussing this topic. As a matter of fact, many people are shunned once they reveal they are gay. We are truly living in times which the Bible describes as a time of right being called wrong and wrong being called right. Lesbianism is a perversion of God's intention for female-to-female interaction.

No, this is not a chapter condemning the woman who has found solace in the arms of another woman. Not at all! To the contrary, it is simply my attempt to expose another "counterfeit method" by which women receive what they perceive as love.

I have personal friends who have engaged this lifestyle. Many people are confused or driven to anger over the topic of lesbian relationships. Still, others are curious as to why women would seek each other to engage in this type of relationship. Consequently, I'm not writing what I think they think. I have open and honest conversations with "my sisters, my friends," and because we create a culture of mutual compassion and sisterly support, I can share an "authentic" perspective with you. So I asked my friends, "What is it about the lesbian experience that is so intoxicating?" The response is below.

My friend shared the following about her intimate relationship with another woman. She (my friend's lover) provides understanding, knowing, sharing, caring and empathy from the inside out. How does this compare to what has been, or to what most say should be? She knows the answers before the questions, the solutions before the problems can be verbalized. Everything concerning me is wrapped up in her. She mentally stimulates me, emotionally comforts me and relates to me. Everything lines up, but most importantly, she doesn't just accept me, she understands me. How fulfilling it is to know that though we just met, she absorbs my pain, heals my wounds and never has to pull out Band-Aids. Knowing that she is around helps me keep my head up because I know all the promises that were broken before will be kept by her because ultimately, she is me.

She drinks and I swallow. If I think it, she says it. If I want it, she buys it. If I cry, her soft touch catches my tears, the water runs down her hand, and she kisses it off. My nose runs and she gently pulls the tissue out of the box and wipes with very little pressure. Something about the way she handles me makes it easier every day to stay just a little while longer. Yeah, it isn't the pick of the crop, as they say. My family is angry at her for indulging me. They can't stand her and she isn't welcomed to the house. Some houses are different and that is what makes it really worth it. Her family welcomes me with open arms and loves me right on in. I get the family initiation. The beauty of it all is that we attend the same church, go to the same club and shop at the same grocery store. I really didn't know she was watching me.

Being friends first in any relationship is a very important attribute and keeps the relationship flourishing. Coming over, spending time and just being concerned about me. Not worried about my body type, telling me I need to lose weight or wear this or that, just loving me for me, and she understands me. She perceives my beauty from within. It is so comforting, with all of my inconsistencies and idiosyncrasies, just to know that she is very consistent and persistent. She is making sure that I get everything I want and, most importantly, everything I need.

All over town you see us. We are everywhere and very visible. Others are turning their noses up while some are too ashamed to join us. Trust me, while you may not think it is noticeable that your eyes are on us, we know that you are looking. The rumors, the curiosity, the flattery is available to us and once you enter, you won't want to escape. Say yes once and you won't really care who knows, unless you're sneaking in and testing the waters. Keep testing and you will find yourself the test. Many are willing to play your game. Easy to get in and can't imagine getting out—this is beautiful.

Something about that "best friend." She knows everything about you already and she is right there when you need her. She knows when you need your nails done, your feet rubbed, and she will send you to the nail spa. She recognizes that you had a hard week and no one understands. Your other friends simply don't care. You can cry on her shoulders and bleed all over her because she was there. She heard and saw the abuse. He was verbally unkind to you. He was emotionally damaging to you, but look who rescued you—your very best friend.

There's something about that coworker who assists you without your asking. She takes you out to lunch knowing that you brought your lunch from home or have money to buy your own lunch. She wants to make sure that all of your projects are completed even if hers may be late. What a concerned friend! She goes out of her way to make sure you achieve your goals and aspirations. She doesn't mind staying overtime with you so you don't have to leave in the dark by yourself. She will spend the night with you so that you are not alone. What a mighty good friend!

These are just some of the reasons why we love each other. These reasons are why it is easy just to hang in there and love the game. The lie is that men think women love women because we have been abused by men. That is not always the case. Possibly it is one of many reasons, but ultimately I am attracted to her. Ultimately, I want to be with her and I don't know why it is such a big deal. When you are rescued it is really easy just to stay. Emotionally, it is so satisfying. Honestly, in my mind is where it all started, and then it moved right into my heart.

Why do we stay, especially with the intensity of the relationship, how is it so binding? We stay because we are one and the same, and we understand the dynamics of the reasons we came together in the first place. There is a marked difference between having a lesbian experience and living the lesbian lifestyle. The experience is *always* sexual. The lifestyle is just living in this culture every day and not wanting anything else.

You are so engulfed with the ties of your emotions. Another thing is that these emotions are intensely different from that of a male-to-female relationship. It's like a magnet. Even if you want to let it go, you can't on your own. These relationships keep you with the guarantee that time will afford you the opportunity again, and you get more and more comfortable as time progresses.

You find yourself craving the relationship and the bond that is formed when two females come together mentally and emotionally. The power of suggestion isn't always with words, it is with gestures and actions that you desire, but it is never vocalized. Love—oh I never knew it like this before! I can't find any man who can satisfy, and really, I am not looking for one. Most of the men I know approve of this relationship anyway, so I don't have to pretend at all with them.

Once you are acclimated to the life, it isn't a struggle to express who you really are. It comes easily and the transition makes you bold and arrogant. Arrogance, by the way, is just another form of insecurity. The attitude is, I don't care how one feels, how one thinks or if this hurts anybody, because it is all about me. Yes, it sounds selfish and it is. The emotional bond is one that can't be described, not in English anyway. It is a bond that is like an infant that nurses from its mother, and you can't get better than that. It's like the knitting of your heart with another heart and it has one beat. The beat is simultaneous and it is always in rhythm. There's something about the passion between us, and it isn't sexual. It's a hidden beauty that evolves in an instant as soon as it is released.

You never know it is on the way. You are just happy with its arrival. You realize that it is really what you have been longing for all the time, and now it is here. The freedom of expression has finally found me. The freedom of just letting go and letting love be alive in my life. The freedom of being assured that in a matter of time, what you didn't know about yourself will soon be revealed. It is real and it is on the rise.

The closet? Not necessary because it isn't obvious, unless you are a trans-dresser. Even then, it is okay because you are still a woman and you know it. Curiosity? Yes, it is inviting when you are wondering, is this happening? How come the couple seems so complete? Yes, it is a matter of time, joining isn't hard to do. You just have to be open. When you are open, it allows IT to come in. IT allows that need to be satisfied, and then you recognize that this is what you needed all the time. IT helps you accept who you are and why you have chosen to love a woman.

Oh, that is lesbianism. It is when you are attracted to women, not just mentally or emotionally, but also sexually. Sex is what makes the relationship stick. No, sex isn't what makes you a lesbian. What you think defines that, but the sexual act determines it.

Same-sex relations between females equal lesbianism. It's so hard to say that word — *lesbianism*. That is what and who we are. Yes, we like relationships with women and sex is a part of that. Talk about a connection that's hard to break! Oh, it isn't going to happen because the sex has now made us one and the same again. My deceptive reality is that she is me and I am her and we are one. A major downfall about the sex part is the jealousy that comes with the relationship. Yes, we are jealous. I hate to admit it, but we are. Will fight you now and take you to dinner later. Will curse you out now and bring flowers to your job. Yes, the experience is intense, but that's why we like it. We like living on the edge. Adventurous — that is exactly what this lesbian thing is between two women. Land on my property and you will pay for it one way or another.

Sharing my friends' perspectives is just doing what I do. I keep it real. I can do that and still love you. If God can draw you to Himself with love and kindness, then so can I. If God can listen to your pain, then so can I. If God can speak life to your broken places, then so can I.

Lesbianism is in church, in your neighborhood, in elementary schools, in middle schools, in high schools, in colleges, on our jobs and in our families. It is real, and for many of the women I know personally who are in this lifestyle, it is a struggle one way or another. This is not about my opinion. It is about my position which is solely based on the Word of God. Lesbianism is counterfeit love.

Life Lessons Learned In This Chapter

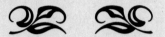

LOVE EMPOWERS US TO LOVE THE WAY GOD ORIGINALLY INTENDED

- Women understand other women with ease.
- Friendship is important to women because women are emotional.
- Frequently, lesbianism is the result of some type of abuse/trauma.
- Lesbian relationships are very difficult to break away from.
- Jealousy/insecurity is an ever-present emotion in lesbian relationships.
- Lesbianism is counterfeit love.

Scripture

But put on the Lord Jesus Christ, and make no provision for the flesh, to fulfill its lusts.

Romans 13:14

Written Affirmation

Share Your Thoughts

I will seek to establish godly, healthy relationships with
other women because:

_____

_____

_____

_____

_____

_____

_____

_____

Faith's Story

BUT HE GOES TO CHURCH
(Spiritual Deception)

Faith met Zach at the church's annual Singles Picnic this past summer. He was a tall, slender young man who often led prayers in Sunday School. He was in the MIT (Ministers in Training) class and was soon going to be addressing the congregation from the pulpit. Zach was a nice guy and the church mothers just loved him. He often helped them to their cars after church and always addressed them with the most Southern manners he could muster up.

Faith was the church secretary and pretty much knew everybody's business but Zach's. You see, he hadn't been at the church a long time. He just showed up one Sunday and has been coming ever since. Zach walked up to Faith one Sunday after service and asked if they could go get something to eat. She agreed and that was the beginning of their relationship. After that, they came to church together and left together. It all began to crumble one day as Faith was walking through the mall behind a group of guys just shooting the breeze. Faith overheard one of the men laughing at how hard Zach Thomas was faking like he loved the Lord in order to marry him a "good church girl."

"That boy is crazy. I don't want a wife and some kids that bad that I would go and pretend to be all into the church the way that fool is doing. He even memorized a book of prayers." One of the other guys said, "And she's a pretty girl too! I think she is the church secretary or something like that. I asked Zach if she had any sisters and he told me just to give him some time. He said he'd have a girl for each of us by the time he got through."

Faith was devastated to say the least. The guys never saw her walking behind them and as soon as she could, she took the nearest exit. "God, thank you for answering my prayer and showing me that Zach was not the one," Faith whispered with tears streaming down her face.

Not only does he go to church, he might be an usher, in the choir, on the security team, a parking lot attendant, a musician, a preacher or a pew member. Yes, he goes to church but does he know your daddy? I am not referring to your biological father—does he know God?

Did you know a lot of men come to church to find a "good woman"? Who is he once he leaves the sanctuary? How does he handle life when the pastor is not around?

The aim of this identification is discipleship, not church attendance. The traits you should look for in a godly man resemble the traits of a learner, follower and imitator of God Himself.

How does he handle money? How does he handle his spiritual life? Does he have a prayer life? Does he have a worship life? Does he handle his finances from a Kingdom perspective? Is he a faithful tither? Does he regularly sow seed into the Kingdom of God? Does he seek to win others to Christ with his lifestyle? Can he lead you as priest, protector and pastor of your home or are you showing him where the book of Exodus is? Does being around him draw you closer to Christ or does it drive a wedge between you and God?

Does being around this man push you into excellence in God? What does he bring to the table? Or is he looking for you to bring the table and set it? Does he celebrate you or tolerate you? What does your pastor or your multitude of counsel think of him? Is he considerate, kind and compassionate? Does he weaken your strengths or strengthen your weaknesses? Let's take it down to the basics. Does he have a prayer life? Does he read, study and meditate on the word of God? Is Christ being formed in him?

Life Lessons Learned In This Chapter

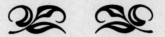

<u>LOVE ASKS LOTS OF QUESTIONS—</u>
<u>THE RIGHT QUESTIONS—</u>
<u>AND PAYS ATTENTION TO THE ANSWERS</u>

- Observe who he is away from church and away from other believers.
- Going to church and knowing God are two different things.
- Relationship with others is only as strong as your fellowship with God.
- Pay attention to other areas of his life (stewardship, attitude, stability).
- Does he draw you closer to God or pull you away from God?
- There's a difference between being religious and having a relationship with God.

Scripture

Even so, every good tree bears good fruit, but a bad tree bears bad fruit. A good tree cannot bear bad fruit, nor can a bad tree bear good fruit. Every tree that does not bear good fruit is cut down and thrown into the fire. Therefore by their fruit you will know them.

Matthew 7:17-20

Written Affirmation

Share Your Thoughts

I will prepare myself not just for a "good choice" but for a "God choice" because:

_____

_____

_____

_____

_____

_____

_____

Diamond's Story

SUGAR DADDIES AREN'T ALWAYS SWEET
(You See Money, He Sees Honey)

After two years of dancing in the club, Diamond was determined that she was not going to work this hard the rest of her life. She decided the next "big spender" that came into the club was going to be exclusively hers. Diamond didn't care if it was the NBA, the NFL, the NBL, a hip-hop star or the most notorious hustler—she was ready to be some man's number one. She scoped the audience every night for what section to spend the most time in.

This must be her lucky night. A group of men came into the club celebrating the "night before a wedding" for one of them. Diamond knew this was her chance to get out of this section of New Jersey. She connected with the spokesperson of the group who offered her $5,000 to do a private show for them. She agreed and got paid more money than she had ever seen in one night. The leader of the group, a well-known businessman, asked Diamond if she was interested in more where that came from. She exclaimed, "Absolutely! What do I have to do?"

He said, "I just want you to be available when I call you and I will give you $5,000 a week plus perks to do whatever I say."

Diamond lived well for the next six months. She was cool with the fact that she had to dance to someone else's music if it meant living like this. She was living in a fully furnished, downtown penthouse condo, driving an S500 Mercedes, and wearing the finest clothes and jewelry. She thought she had died and gone to heaven until the police showed up at her door at 6:00 a.m. one cold winter morning. Her dreams were over quicker than they had started when her man's wife entered after the police to have her arrested for trespassing. Mrs. Big Spender calmly said, "This is my house. My next stop is our mansion across town to serve Mr. Big Baller his divorce papers. He has lost his mind if he thinks he is going to squander my inheritance away like this. You can have him, but you can't have my stuff!" I guess everything that glitters is not gold!

I'm not saying you are a gold-digger…but you only consider men with money, certain career status or who you perceive to have money and certain career status. Stop looking for a man to give you the life you dream about. Set goals, create a plan, work the plan and create your own satisfaction. Confident, secure, well-balanced women attract confident, secure, well-balanced men.

I love to read. On one occasion while I was reading a magazine several years ago, I came across a quote from one of the most profound thinkers and writers of our time. Nikki Giovanni said, "Deal with yourself as an individual worthy of respect and make everyone else deal with you the same way." That has stuck with me and has been a constant motivation in my life in terms of how I interact with others.

I've been blessed with great friends. I have one friend who has a story for everything. This friend has yet to answer one of my questions with a yes or no. The answer always comes in the form of an illustration. I've come to accept that it is a great way to receive wisdom. One day we were discussing a situation where we felt the people involved needed to be patient instead of anxious. I was simply asking for advice on how to address the issue. My friend said, "You can't be a whore today and a prostitute tomorrow." I said, "What?" My friend reiterated that if a man gets it (sex, time, attention, etc.) for free today, why would he pay for it tomorrow? I thought, "Wow!"

As women, we give so much away without any reciprocity. We get nothing in return of any significant value.

Many women are trained at a young age to be gold-diggers. If they have a certain look (hair, complexion, figure), they know how to work those attributes to their advantage. These women are encouraged to pursue a man who is very wealthy (professional athlete, doctor, lawyer, stockbroker) and even go as far as attending or hanging out at the same schools or venues in an attempt to become a part of Mr. Right's life in one way or another. Sometimes the thinking is: If I can't marry him I'll have his baby and be connected to him for the next eighteen years. No, this is not all women. However, let's be honest here and acknowledge that such women do exist.

For each of us, our deepest longing and desire as a woman is to be loved. Somehow, we have been tricked into believing that we must be manipulative, deceitful, cunning and dishonest to get stuff. Stuff is for people who have no vision, no dreams or desires beyond the present moment.

Okay, so he is a great man because he buys you jewelry, gets your hair and nails done weekly, pays your bills, takes you to dinner whenever you like for some steak and seafood, lets you drive his fancy car, and takes you on trips. He is also a great listener and a strong shoulder to cry on. Put your face close to the page so I can love-smack you back into reality.

Having his baby does not secure your future either. Yes, many women foolishly attempt to trap (and some succeed) their ideal "money man" by getting pregnant with his child. Rarely, and I do mean rarely, does this result in you and the baby's father building a healthy family living happily ever after. This frequently creates more problems and eventual heartache for you. Do you know that a significant number of pregnant women are murdered each year by the baby's father in an attempt to get rid of "the problem." My point here is that this is not only foolish, it is extremely dangerous.

It is also necessary for me to mention here that often the public persona and the private realities of sugar daddies are usually *very* different. How do you know he really has what he claims? Are you sure he is not "asset-sitting" for a well-to-do friend, associate or employer? Is it possible that he has a family member who works for a rental car company that specializes in luxury vehicles? Why can't you have his home number *and* his cell number?

Superficial pursuits produce superficial results. Chasing a man for his money may be exciting at first. However, I assure you this adventure will begin to cost you something you are not willing to pay for the rest of your life.

You must be willing to accept his other relationships without rocking the boat. You must be willing to make yourself available whenever he wants you, and, at least in his mind, you are restricted from pursuing or engaging in other intimate associations.

If you really want to know where you and Mr. Sugar Daddy stand, stop having sex with him and see what is left. You are a toy. Just as children are excited on Christmas morning with all the new gifts under the tree and are bored by the middle of January (if that long), Mr. Sugar Daddy will be looking for his next plaything soon too. That does not necessarily mean he will replace you just yet. Frequently, he just adds you to his list of women and then begins to schedule you according to his plans for the week, month or year. You are not for sale. Choose a man for who he is and not for what he has. If you get your soul (emotions) together you can get your life together.

Life Lessons Learned In This Chapter

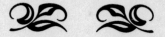

<u>THE LOVE OF MONEY IS THE ROOT OF ALL EVIL</u>

- Women give too much away without reciprocity.
- Superficial pursuits produce superficial results.
- Deal with a man based on his character and not based on what you think you can get from him.
- All that glitters is not gold—some of it is just polished metal.

Scripture

Better is a little with the fear of the Lord than great treasure with trouble.

Proverbs 15:16

Written Affirmation

Share Your Thoughts

I will not be driven by money in relationships because:

_____

_____

_____

_____

_____

_____

_____

_____

Niko's Story

WHO IS THAT?
(Jealousy/Insecurity)

Niko was beginning to feel the loathing that always came when he realized that he should have listened to his mother. She'd always told him that a clingy, needy woman was more trouble than she was worth. When his parents came to Indianapolis to visit him, he was excited that they could spend time with his new official girlfriend Taylor. She seemed to have it all together. The final test prior to potential long-term commitment was for his mother to give her the once-over as only another woman can. They hadn't really hit it off too well during his mother's brief visit last month. Niko's mom had told him to get away from Taylor quickly because she had a "not-so-good" feeling about her.

This time his younger sister Jasmine unexpectedly came along as well, which, for Niko, was a pleasant surprise. He hadn't seen Jasmine since she and her husband moved to Hawaii a year and a half earlier.

Niko and his parents had gone to the grocery store, leaving Jasmine at his place to rest. She was still tired from the long flight to her parents before the six-hour drive to see her brother. Taylor called shortly after the family left and Jazz, as her brother nicknamed her, answered the phone. However, whoever was on the other end said nothing prior to hanging up. As the family returned home, they pulled up just in time to see Taylor slicing Niko's tires and spray-painting the word cheater on his black car with white paint. His parents were speechless. Niko jumped out of the car and ran over to Taylor asking her what was wrong with her. Her response, "Nobody cheats on me and gets away with it. Another woman answered your phone and I knew it wasn't your mother because I saw you all at the grocery store."

"I should have listened to my mother the first time," he said. "You are crazy, and as of this moment, this relationship is over—forever. That was my sister who answered my phone."

As Taylor stood there looking bewildered and staring at the can of paint in her hand, her future walked away toward his front door and didn't bother to look back.

The Bible says in Isaiah 44:2 that we were in the care of God before we were born. Consequently, He knew us before we knew ourselves and He is the only one who can tell us what we are worth. Until we know our worth, based on God's word, we will not know whether we are in love or in need. As soon as someone gives us consistent attention, we become clingy, needy and possessive.

From the beginning of time, jealousy has led to the destruction of kingdoms, and has been the downfall of many men and women. It has been called a contradictory and chaotic passion. It can turn feelings of profound sadness and fear into restless distress, unbearable humiliation and shocking hostility. Experts say jealousy is an obvious sign of insecurity. The struggle with jealousy is really a search for significance. We know we want more. We just are not sure where to find it.

According to Dr. Shirley Glass, a clinical psychologist and member of the American Association for Marriage and Family Therapy, "Jealous women are constantly comparing themselves to others and are often very sour people."

In order to reverse the pangs of jealousy, people need to change their focus of control from external to internal. Instead of focusing or being swayed by things outside, reclaim control by moving toward self-actualization or self-fulfillment so you do not feel so deprived by what others have. In other words—*get a life!*

How do you find life? You must first find unconditional love. When God is not involved in the process of loving, we deflect the very thing we attract. We lack the capacity to trust others because we cannot trust ourselves. When you attempt your definition of love without God's help, you place impossible demands on people who are close to you because you are your only focus and you want to be their only focus too.

You frustrate, intimidate and manipulate people because you are so tied to "self" in an attempt to avoid rejection rather than embracing love. You try to earn love by pleasing people, and when that does not work you retreat in anger and become accusatory of everyone who will not focus on your pain. If you want to become more attractive decide to be less needy. Psalm 84:11 promises us that no good thing will He withhold from you if you walk upright before Him. Proverbs 16:25 gives us a nugget to live by. It says, "Understanding is a wellspring of life to him or her who has it."

A really functional "mature" relationship will be characterized by the lack of emphasis on issues about power or control. Instead, both the partners will feel closely connected while maintaining a strong sense of individuality and independence within the relationship. This is how relationships are meant to be. In this type of relationship, there is a high level of trust, mutual respect and friendship.

You always have options and you are in control of your life. Make different choices and you will get different results. There is no need to be jealous of anyone for anything. What God has for you is for you. Realize right now that all of your needs are met and your sense of self-worth comes from God. Now get yourself together so that God can release your stuff. The only thing green you want attached to you is money!

Life Lessons Learned In This Chapter

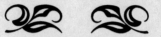

<u>LOVE IS PATIENT AND NOT RUDE</u>

- Jealous women are constantly comparing themselves to others.
- Reclaim control of your life by moving toward self-fulfillment.
- Finding unconditional love in God is the key to releasing jealousy.
- What God has for you is for you.
- The only thing green you want attached to you is money.

Scripture

Become complete. Be of good comfort, be of one mind, live in peace; and the God of love and peace will be with you.

2 Corinthians 13:11

Written Affirmation

Share Your Thoughts

I will not exhibit jealousy or insecurity in my relationships because:

_____

_____

_____

_____

_____

_____

_____

Tracie's Story

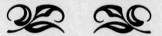

WILL THE REAL YOU PLEASE STAND UP
(The Great Pretender)

Tracie was always trying to impress people. It seemed that her life's mission was to overspend, overcommit and under-deliver—especially when it came to being genuine. It was important to Tracie to be perceived as a woman of wealth and power with a hint of arrogance. When we first met, she presented herself to everyone as a woman who had a lot of money. She went looking for new homes in the priciest neighborhoods and always went car-shopping at luxury car dealerships. The strange thing about Tracie's habits was that she had neither a job nor a traceable form of income that could afford her this level of living. She spent hours walking through Macy's, Neiman's, Blooming-dales and Saks. She was forever name-dropping to let us all know that she spent time with the rich and famous.

It was exciting to her small-town girlfriends—until we found out how she met these people. Tracie had a part-time job on the weekends as a server for a major catering company about an hour away that only serviced high-end clients. Tracie had worked for this company for the last two years and made a decent living. However, she was not making enough money to drive the car she was driving, wear the designer clothes and jewelry she often flaunted, and to eat at the five-star restaurants she treated us to on occasion. You see, in addition to her position as a server, Tracie had another part-time job during the week as a house-sitter. She told us she was into real estate and investments.

The thing is, we didn't really care what she did. We just enjoyed her company whenever she could join us for our monthly tea-and-talk time. One Friday evening as we were enjoying our girlfriend time at Jason's Jazz Café, the covers came flying off her façade. A woman for whom she had been house-sitting came into the restaurant and spoke to Tracie. Of particular note was how she took the time to thank Tracie for cleaning her house, washing her car and getting her clothes from the dry cleaners while she was on vacation. The look on Tracie's face was sheer embarrassment!

It's just easier to be you. It is exhausting to have to figure out who you want to pretend to be on a daily basis to impress people who are not thinking about you that much anyway.

You should take full advantage of being a woman. However, external beauty without internal emotional balance is fertile ground for chaotic relationships. Pretending to be something you are not and deferring to other people's preferences to try and get them to like you is not a healthy way to pursue love! The reason is that the "real you" will always eventually come out.

When you hide the real you in a relationship, this becomes a counterfeit relationship. Respect should be the core element between any two people, and to be dishonest in the beginning makes way for eventual breakdown and ultimate destruction. Men thrive on respect. When you enter a relationship on false pretenses, disrespect is inevitable. You cannot have long-term respect for people you deceive.

When others feel good about you, you are popular. However, when you feel good about yourself, you are successful. When you are authentically walking in the steps God created for you, you will perpetually experience the highest level of joy within. This is possible because your joy is no longer predicated on your context (what is happening around you), but is based on your content (the power that is working in you). Make God's opinion the source of your self-worth.

In her book, *In the Meantime*, Iyanla Vanzant says, "When we have hidden agendas, unclear motives, unachievable fantasies, dishonesty, and false responsibilities as the basis of a relationship, it is a safe bet that there is no love present. What is present may look like love, feel like love, but is not, in any way, shape, form or fashion, even closely related to the essence of love.

"You cannot do what absolutely makes no sense and call it love. When you are willing to tell one lie after another lie after another lie, when you sneak, hide, and deceive, when you do to someone the very thing you would not want done to you, you are not in pursuit of love. You are acting out your mental garbage and emotional trash."

That is not who we are as women. We were created to be who we are and who we are is equipped to stand the test of time. You were created to shine. You were created to rise. That's what women do — *we rise!*

As builders of communities and dreams — we rise. We rise because women are multipliers. Whatever you give to us — we cause it to increase. If you give us a seed of life, we will produce a baby. If you give us an apple — we will make pie. Women take little and stretch it to become enough — because we are designed and wired to rise. If you give us love — we will flourish. Consequently, if you mishandle us — we will multiply the pain, confusion and distortion until another woman comes along to build us back up again. Why? Because as women — *we rise!*

Eleanor Roosevelt said, "Throughout history women have been forced to make adjustments. The result is that in most cases, it is less difficult for a woman to adapt to new situations than it is for a man." Women have a tremendous spirit of adaptability.

Consequently, over time, women have proven that building anything — be it dreams, communities, family, careers—requires standing on the shoulders of those who have come before us. Women like Eleanor Roosevelt, Mary McLeod Bethune, Susan B. Anthony, Coretta Scott King, Elizabeth Williams, your mothers, grandmothers, teachers and neighbors, all helped to shape you into the person you are still becoming. Each generation prepares for the next. The result—*we rise!*

With any building project there are many roles. From the land developer to the architect to the plumber to the electrician to the interior designer—each person's contribution is critical to the success of the finished product. That's what makes "woman" so special. Some women purchased the land with their lives. They suffered for us to have much of what we enjoy today. Some women have laid the foundation by establishing a solid base upon which we live. Still other women work on the infrastructure that includes our hopes, dreams and culture.

Not all of these roles get recognized, yet they are still important. Some are out front—some are behind the scenes. Some of the women who filled these roles are known, some unknown. Some black, some white, some Hispanic, some educated, some skilled, some married, some widowed, some civilian, some military, but all are women and still *we rise*.

I am honored to be a woman who now walks through doors, stands on floors and enjoys opportunities created by the labor of our foremothers. Wherever you are in your pursuit of fulfillment, know that you have something unique and valuable to deposit into the lives of others as you continue to build communities and dreams. Because when the going gets tough—what do we do as women? *WE RISE!*

Life Lessons Learned In This Chapter

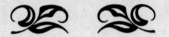

<u>LOVE IS HONEST ALL THE TIME—</u>
<u>NO MATTER WHAT</u>

- Pretending to be something you are not is unhealthy.
- Honesty and respect are core elements of any relationship.
- You cannot have long-term respect for people you deceive.
- Men thrive on respect.
- You were created to shine.

Scripture

There is a way that seems right to man, but its end is the way of destruction.

Proverbs 16:25

Written Affirmation

Share Your Thoughts

I will seek to be authentic in my relationships because:

_____

_____

_____

_____

_____

_____

_____

Hope's Story

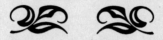

AND THE WINNER IS...
(Drama Queen)

My friend Hope and her boyfriend Nathan were always arguing or angry about something. It seemed that the more dramatic Hope became, the more passionate their relationship was. While Nathan frequently complained about Hope's behavior, he never did anything differently except take a break from the drama. Hope knew that Nathan would always come back because he always had. Sometimes their separation would last for months. Then, out of the blue, they would be seen together walking down the street holding hands.

A group of us started gambling on the relationship, taking bets regarding how long they would actually get along each time they reconciled. We all stopped listening to their lamentations because we realized that it wasn't going to change anything. They would always end up back together.

Hope overreacts to everything. It's always about how the situation or circumstances are going to affect her and her world. She is basically one of the most selfish, self-centered people I know and I tolerate her because I feel sorry for her. She can be *really pitiful at times. At other times she can be one of the meanest people ever. Still, she can be helpful—mostly when it will benefit her. She rarely thinks before she speaks and never considers how her words will cut you. She just has to get it out. I'm really afraid for Hope because I often warn her that one day she is going to meet her match and truly get her feelings hurt or worse.*

In the meantime, Nathan continues to be her yo-yo with his codependent behavior. Somehow he has convinced himself that they can't live without each other or with each other, so they will continue just to do the best they can.

Humans are social creatures and need social interaction, feedback and validation of their self-worth. Most of us receive this naturally from our daily lives. However, people with low self-esteem and low self-confidence are frequently insecure. Consequently, they spend a lot of time creating situations in which they become the center of attention. This behavior only provides temporary relief. Drama queens often display bullying behaviors that include manipulation, tantrums, lying and deception all to avoid being exposed.

Some drama queens seek over-the-top attention by exploiting the suffering of other people. Still others feign suffering to manipulate people's emotions. Then there is the drama queen who always comes to the rescue just in the nick of time. When not in rescue mode, the drama queen may be resentful because there is nothing for her to do.

It is serious—but never that serious. You missed your calling. You should be in Hollywood going from audition to audition. You are so talented and should maximize your gift because you specialize in exploiting, exaggerating and elevating details to proportions beyond belief. My girlfriend advice to you is simply to take a deep breath and calm down.

I am exaggerating the issue, not to make fun of you, but to help you acknowledge that you deserve better than the worst you can stand. I know what it is to embrace abnormal as normal. I know what it is to be so comfortable with chaos that peace makes you uncomfortable.

One of my favorite authors, Mike Murdock, said, "Many thrive on strife. They destroy anything they cannot own or control. Peace is boring, peace makes them sick, and warfare is their lifeline." That is just too much energy to invest in a relationship that bears nothing but pain.

Another word for this type of behavior is *narcissism*. Narcissists are people who overestimate their abilities, inflate their accomplishments, devalue the achievements and accomplishments of others and react angrily to criticism.

People with this type of personality have trouble recognizing the needs and feelings of those around them, are dismissive, contemptuous, impatient and oblivious to the hurtful things they say to others.

Drama is not the way to get and keep healthy relationships. Being happy, confident and content are the ingredients of wholesome interaction. Productive and balanced women excite productive and balanced men. Being dramatic is draining — both to you and to the people who must deal with you. Real love, true love, God love should energize and excite you. It should not exhaust and exasperate you.

In her book, *Women Who Love Too Much*, Robin Norwood states, "If the relationship we have with our parents was essentially a nurturing one, with appropriate expressions of affection, interest, and approval, then as adults we tend to feel comfortable with people who engender similar feelings of security, warmth, and positive self-regard. Further, we will tend to avoid people who make us feel less positive. However, if our parents related to us in hostile, critical, cruel, manipulative, overbearing, overdependent, or otherwise inappropriate ways, that is what will feel right to us when we meet someone who expresses perhaps very similar undertones of the same attitudes and behaviors.

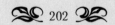

"If drama and chaos have always been present in our lives, and if, as is so often the case, we were forced to deny many of our own feelings while growing up, we often require dramatic events to engender any feelings at all. Thus, we need the excitement of uncertainly, pain, disappointment, and struggle just to feel alive."

People in drama-filled relationships stay in them because the pain of being alone is worse than the greatest pain the relationship produces. The key is in learning how to live a healthy, satisfying and serene life without being dependent on another person for happiness. Find a way to trade excitement connected to turmoil for the lasting joy of a deeper, peaceful intimacy.

Life Lessons Learned In This Chapter

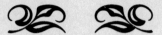

<u>LOVE IS NOT FULL OF TURMOIL</u>

- Many people thrive on strife.
- Some people destroy what they cannot control.
- Drama is not the way to get and keep healthy relationships.
- We tend to find serenity in what is familiar—even if that is drama.
- Real, true God love should energize you—not drain you.

Scripture

And let the peace of God rule in your hearts.

Colossians 3:15

Written Affirmation

Share Your Thoughts

I will seek peace and undisturbed composure in my relationships because:

_____

_____

_____

_____

_____

_____

_____

Veronica's Story

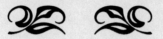

AIN'T NOTHING LIKE THE REAL THING
(Love Is...)

They met at her cousin's wedding in the Bahamas. There was definitely "something" at first sight between them. We are still not sure if it was attraction, intrigue or curiosity.

Veronica was a bridesmaid and one of the sweetest people ever. It was amazing to those of us who knew Veronica how strong and resilient she was. Just three years earlier when she was just thirty-one, she had lost her husband and infant daughter in a terrible car accident. That's why she moved back to Denver from Memphis to be with her family. Veronica knew the only way to be able to keep living without her childhood sweetheart and baby girl was to let God heal her and turn her sorrow into strength. She started a support group for women who have lost family members to sudden death.

Vance was a strong-looking, gentle-natured guy who was the best man. He and his five brothers grew up with the groom. Vance was thirty-seven and had never been married before. At the reception, Veronica and Vance danced together the entire evening and everyone could see that another spark had been lit.

It was the beginning of an unbelievable friendship. Although she lived in Denver and Vance lived in Baltimore, their friendship blossomed during the next year because Vance was an airline pilot for a major company. On his days off, he would fly to Denver just to take Veronica to dinner and spend time with her and her family.

Veronica was a middle-school English teacher. She was also very active as a mentor for young ladies at her church. They talked every day, prayed together, spent holidays together, and shared their dreams with each other. They agreed to remain celibate during their courtship and at times, temptation almost got the best of them. They postulated that if they could remain faithful to God during this time, then remaining faithful to each other would not be a challenge.

Everyone assumed another wedding was on the horizon. They were right. During one of his visits to Denver, Vance went to church with Veronica to ask her pastor, who was also her father, for her hand in marriage. After six months of premarital counseling and working out his job transfer to Denver, it was time for another wedding celebration. That was the beginning of twenty years of heaven on earth.

They still call each other "sweetheart." He is still kind to Veronica and her heart is still tender toward Vance. Their love has endured the death of his mother and her father. Their love has produced three beautiful children and one grandchild is on the way. Their love has endured Vance's prostate cancer scare and Veronica's breast cancer treatment. Their love has built a dream home in Denver and bought a vacation home in the islands that gave birth to their love — the Bahamas. Their love has established a trust fund for their children and is prepared to care for their aging parents. Their love has been a refuge for other married couples needing advice. Their love has been challenged at times and stretched to the limit. They have endured, however, because real love conquers all. Real love is patient and kind. The beauty of their love is that they love each other more today than they did when they first realized it was a match made in heaven. Love is not a feeling. Love is a choice. Love is a commitment. Real love wins every time!

*G*od wants to turn your story of disaster, despair and devastation into a testimony of discovery, determination and destiny. Your life is so much larger than your intentions. However, in order to embrace this wonderful and beautiful place, you must recognize that the love of God is not an ordinary love.

To paraphrase what the Bible says in 1 John 3:

1   See what an incredible quality of love the Father has bestowed on us, that we should be called the children of God! And so we are! The reason that the world does not know (recognize, acknowledge) us is that it does not know Him.

2   Beloved, we are now God's children; it is not yet disclosed what we shall be hereafter, but we know that when He comes and is manifested, we shall be like Him, for we shall see Him just as He is.

3   And everyone who has this hope in Him cleanses or purifies himself just as He is pure.

The love God wants us to experience must be found in and through Him. His love for me is perfect and is based on Him, not based on me. Therefore, even when I mess up on purpose or make an honest mistake, He keeps on loving me no matter what. This is a critical point because God's love is key in our emotional healing.

Paraphrasing once again what Paul says in Ephesians 2:

4   But God—so rich is He in His mercy! Because of and in order to satisfy the great and wonderful and intense love with which He loved us,

5   Even when we were slain by our own shortcom-

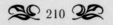 210

ings and trespasses, He made us alive together in fellowship and in union with Christ; it is by grace that you are saved,

6 And He raised us up together with Him and made us sit down together in the heavenly sphere in Christ Jesus.

I had an experience several years ago that increased my compassion for people who are disconnected and do not know it. I was walking through a grocery store and encountered someone I had not seen in a long time. When this person and I saw each other, I was ready to embrace the person, but was met with a very cold and callous demeanor which clearly said to me, "I wish you had not seen me because I really do not want to talk to you." Initially, I was intimidated and almost stopped in my tracks.

However, it felt as though an angel was behind me pushing me toward the person to speak anyway. I greeted the person, who went through the mechanics of communicating, showing no emotion whatsoever. As I walked away, instead of feeling angry, I felt extreme pity and sadness. The Lord instructed me to keep that person in prayer. He said to me, "Vikki, people cannot give to you what they do not possess." That was an "Ah-ha" space of truth for me because in that very moment, I was set free from the spirit of rejection.

As we understand from the Bible in 1 John 4:

7 Beloved, let us love one another, for love springs from God; and he who loves his fel-

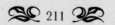

lows is born of God and is coming to know and understand God.

8 He who does not love does not and never did know God, for God is love.

9 The love of God was made manifest where we are concerned in that God sent His Son, His only begotten Son, into the world so that we might live through Him.

10 In this is love: not that we loved God, but that He loved us and sent His Son to be the propitiation—the atoning sacrifice—for our sins.

11 Beloved, if God loved us so very much, we ought also to love one another.

12 No man has at any time yet seen God. But if we love one another, God abides in us, and His love is perfected in us.

13 By this we come to know that we abide in Him and He in us: because He has given to us of His Holy Spirit.

14 And besides we ourselves have seen and bear witness that the Father has sent the Son as the Savior of the world.

15 Anyone who confesses that Jesus is the Son of God, God lives in him and he abides in God.

16 And we know and believe the love God cherishes for us. God is love, and he who dwells and continues in love dwells and continues in God, and God dwells and continues in him.

17 In this union and communion with Him, love is brought to completion and attains perfection, that we may have confidence for the day of judg-

ment, with assurance and boldness to face Him, because as He is, so are we in this world.

18 There is no fear in love, but perfect love turns out fear and expels every trace of terror! For fear brings with it the thought of punishment, and so he who is afraid has not reached the full maturity of love nor is he yet grown into love's complete perfection.

19 We love Him, because He first loved us.

20 If anyone says, I love God, and hates his brother, he is a liar; for he who does not love his brother, whom he has seen, cannot love God, Whom he has not seen.

21 And this commandment we have from Him: that he who loves God shall love his brother also.

Our definition of love is quite different from God's definition of love. The love of God is a radical and life-changing force that causes us to come into existence. Once you become, you produce. The key to finding security, which is what the little girl in all of us desires, is finding significance.

To paraphrase the Bible in 1 Corinthians 13:

4 Love endures long and is patient and kind; love never is envious nor boils over with jealousy, is not boastful or vainglorious, does not display itself haughtily.

5 It is not conceited; it is not rude and does not act unbecomingly. Love does not insist on its own rights or its own way, for it is not self-seeking; it is not fretful or resentful; it takes no account of the evil done to it.

6   It does not rejoice at injustice and unrighteous-
    ness, but rejoices when right and truth prevail.

7   Love bears up under anything and everything
    that comes, is ever ready to believe the best of
    every person, its hopes are fadeless under all cir-
    cumstances, and it endures everything without
    weakening.

8   Love never fails. As for prophecy—the gift of in-
    terpreting the divine will and purpose—it will be
    fulfilled and pass away; as for tongues, they will
    be destroyed and cease; as for knowledge, it will
    pass.

The love of God for me never stops. God created us for
love. Sin separated us from God so He had to send His
only begotten Son into the world to save it so that He
could redeem us back to Himself. What manner of love is
this that a man would lay down his life for us? If you can
believe that God loves you perfectly, then you can believe
that you are worth loving. You are accepted as the beloved
of God. Once you accept this truth, you will be able to love
God and love people the way God intended.

Paraphrasing once again, from Romans 8:

35 Who shall ever separate us from Christ's love?
    Shall suffering and affliction and tribulation? Or
    calamity and distress? Or persecution or hunger
    or destitution or peril or sword?

36 Even as it is written, For Thy sake we are put to
    death all the day long; we are regarded and
    counted as sheep for the slaughter.

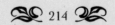

37 Yet amid all these things we are more than con-
   querors, and gain a surpassing victory through
   Him Who loved us.

38 For I am persuaded beyond doubt that neither
   death nor life, nor angels nor principalities, nor
   things impending and threatening nor things to
   come, nor powers,

39 Nor height nor depth, nor anything else in all
   creation will be able to separate us from the love
   of God which is in Christ Jesus our Lord.

God's love for me cannot be measured. However, once
I tap into His love, I enter a realm of living life with no
limits.

As I understand Ephesians 3 to mean:

14 For this reason — seeing the greatness of this plan
   by which you are built together in Christ — I bow
   my knees before the Father of our Lord Jesus
   Christ,

15 For Whom every family in heaven and on earth
   is named.

16 May He grant you out of the rich treasury of His
   glory to be strengthened and reinforced with
   mighty power in the inner man by the Holy Spirit
   Himself, dwelling in your innermost being and
   personality.

17 May Christ through your faith actually dwell in
   your hearts! May you be rooted deep in love and
   founded securely on love,

18 That you may have the power and be strong to

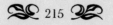

apprehend and grasp with all the saints what is the breadth and length and height and depth of it;

19 That you may really come to know the love of Christ, which far surpasses mere knowledge; that you may be filled through all your being unto all the fullness of God, filled and flooded with God Himself!

20 Now to Him Who, by the power that is at work within us, is able to do superabundantly, far over and above all that we dare ask or think,

21 To Him be glory in the church and in Christ Jesus throughout all generations forever and ever. Amen.

God is the real thing. Every time you see *love*, insert *God*. He says what He means and means what He says. He loves us truly and knows us deeply. Psalm 62:1 states "In Him alone my soul waits." God is the perfection of affection. His ways are not our ways and His thoughts are not our thoughts. God is going to do everything He said He would do. However, quite frequently it's not the way we thought it would happen.

While I was gathering information and being open to divine inspiration for this book, God gave me a five-fold model for love relationships. The Bible speaks of the purpose of the five-fold ascension ministry gifts in Ephesians 4:11-16:

And He Himself gave some to be apostles, some prophets, some pastors and teachers, for the equipping of the saints, For the work of ministry, for the edifying of the body of Christ, Till we all come to the unity of the faith and of the knowledge of the Son of God, to be a perfect man, to the measure of the stature of the fullness of Christ; That we should no longer be children, tossed to and fro and carried about with every wind of doctrine, by the trickery of men, in the cunning craftiness of deceitful plotting, But speaking the truth in love, may grow up in all things into Him who is the head — Christ — And from whom the whole body, joined and knit together by what every joint supplies, according to the effective working by which every part does its share, causes growth of the body for the edifying of itself in love.

Wow! That is so powerful! The model, when each component works together as one unit, causes maturity, wisdom and progress in the spirit of love.

I want to expound briefly upon the role of each ministry gift so that you understand the revelation of the five-fold model for love relationships. Specifically, (1) the Apostle (governs), (2) the Prophet (guides), (3) the Evangelist (gathers), (4) the Pastor (guards), and (5) the Teacher (grows). This paradigm is a pattern that is consistent throughout scripture and established for our protection.

Hence, another pattern of God for our relational growth is (1) salvation, (2) prayer life/word study, (3) communion with God, (4) order in your life, and (5) worship.

When it comes to love the way God intended, prayerfully embrace the following Model of Progression in Love

Relationships: (1) *friendship*—which is for character observation, (2) *open communication*—which is for information gathering and (3) *intimacy*—which comes from establishing a friendship that has open communication. This phase is characterized by honesty with safety. (4) *finances*—which speaks to trust and security in a relationship and (5) *sex*—which is the ultimate pleasure of God-ordained relationships.

When the order of the Model of Progression in Love Relationships is reversed, it becomes fertile ground for counterfeit love. For example—and particularly for women—when the relationship begins with *premature sexual encounters*, the next best thing to expect is some *financial support* (hair salon visits, manicures, pedicures, bills paid, vacations, shopping sprees, spending money) as an indication that he appreciates your making available your body for his needs. Certainly you are not having sex for money but it ultimately turns into that whether we like it or not.

Next, a longing for *intimacy* begins to creep through your chaotic emotions, because now it feels as though you are being used for sexual gratification devoid of any meaning at all. Eventually your complaint becomes that the two of you never *communicate* but only come together for sex, and you begin to feel used. Finally, you desire to be *friends* and he is not genuinely interested because to him you are only good for sex.

Real love does not need a reason—it just is. Real love is forever—it does not stop. Real love is a decision and is sacrificial. Love gives and gives and gives. Real love forgives and keeps no account of wrong. Real love allows

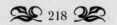

freedom and affirms the unique value of the one loved. Real love is not afraid to lose because this kind of love avoids power struggles.

Real love is without restraint, rules or regulations that restrict. Real love causes expansion, exposure and excitement. We have all heard before, "If you love something set it free. If it comes back to you it is yours. If it does not come back to you it never was." Real love returns every time.

Real love is full of compassion, courage and compliments. Real love complements the object of its affection. Real love is the concrescence of two hearts and two lives.

A close friend shared with me the story of a couple who had a phenomenal friendship, courtship and marriage. The couple had established a solid, long-term friendship. Not wanting to "cross the line" out of fear of destroying the friendship, the young lady rejected her friend's attempts to advance the relationship. Frustrated by her fear, one day he was touched by an angel and said, "Just let me love you. By the time I am finished loving you, you will have learned how to love me back." Whoa! That's what I'm talking about right there. Is that not wonderful?

They were already long-term friends so a long engagement was not necessary. It was a quick engagement, wedding and marriage. Shortly after the wedding, the husband suddenly died in his sleep with his pregnant wife next to him. Yes, she was devastated. However, God's grace sustained her and she is now happy and in love again.

God loves us just like that. He comes quietly, is patient while we work through our issues, transforms us, estab-

lishes us and then changes our lives forever. Nobody can love us like God can—absolutely no one.

Christian author Paula Rinehart said, "Getting to know God is mostly about letting Him in. It's about letting ourselves be loved by Him and giving over to Him the things that fascinated us while they stole our very life, offering us no true sweetness and no real joy."

To paraphrase the way Jeremiah describes the wonder of God's love in Jeremiah 31:3:

> The Lord appeared of old to me (Israel), saying, Yes, I have loved you with an everlasting love; therefore with loving-kindness have I drawn you and continued My faithfulness to you.

God loves us into our rightful place.

Life is all about love. Love is the only true meaning of life. Being alive means that we live in love's house and are accountable to love's rules. Neither life nor love require us to give up our dignity, self-worth, career objective, favorite activities or our good common sense.

Unfortunately, many of us have heretofore believed that it was necessary to give up one thing or another in order to receive love. We were oblivious to the fact that the highest expression of love is the realization and expression of more—more of who you are, more of what you do, more of what you believe, and more of what you have. Love has the ability to bring all of you together, at one time, as one experience, and produce life. That was and still is God's original pattern of love.

We do many foolish things in the name of love. We

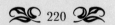

attempt to create love with others before first allowing God to create love within us. You cannot get love on the outside until you have experienced love on the inside. Consequently, we do many things for the sake of love— often loving by trial and error.

We like people for who they are. However, love speaks to who *we* are. We are able to love people not because they are loveable, but because we possess the capacity to love. We can never do enough, fast enough, for enough people, in enough situations to receive from them the love, acceptance, admiration and approval we seem to need. This can only be found in a true, pure, honest relationship with God. We consistently look for love in all the wrong places, not realizing that we must bring love with us.

Jesus says in John 13:

34 I give you a new commandment: that you should love one another. Just as I have loved you, so you too should love one another.
35 By this shall all men know that you are My disciples, if you love one another.

God has already given us love with no strings attached. Love is not about survival. Love is about growth. If you are not growing then you are not loving and being loved. If you are not experiencing love then you are not experiencing God. John 3:16 tells us that "God so loved the world that He gave His only begotten Son." God gave…

God is still giving today. God wants to captivate you with His combination of mystery, majesty and meekness. He wants to be embraced as the lover of your soul. He desires intimacy with you beyond your flesh. God wants to know your innermost self. Intimacy is the ability to be yourself completely in the presence of someone else. Oh how He loves you! Oh how He desires to manifest His great love toward you!

Life Lessons Learned In This Chapter

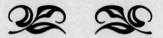

LOVE CAUSES YOU TO GROW

- The love of God is radical and life-changing.
- The love of God is based on who He is—not who I am.
- God created us for love and His love cannot be measured.
- Real love is without restraint.
- Real love is about commitment and responsibility.

Scripture

This is My commandment, that you love one another as I have loved you.

John 15:12

Written Affirmation

Share Your Thoughts

I am only open to authentic and affirming love relationships because:

_____

_____

_____

_____

_____

_____

_____

One of My Stories—I Have Many

KEEP SHOWING UP FOR LOVE

*L*ove is a beautiful thing. As far back as I can remember I have been what some may call a hopeless romantic. I love love. I love to watch people in love. I enjoy love songs. I get excited when people I love find love. Sometimes my love of love has gotten me into difficult situations. I have reasoned that this is because I have so much love to give and to share. I just needed the Lord to teach me how to govern my love properly so that it always brought Him glory. We all stumble and occasionally fall. The key to being a winner is to keep getting up after you fall and to keep showing up for this thing called love.

I have been blessed by love. I have great friendships with both men and women. I have been touched by love. Some of my romantic encounters have caused me to grow tremendously in areas where I thought my capacity was full. I have loved and lost love. I have been betrayed by others who didn't understand the nature of love. I have been loved so much by someone that his love for me caused him to walk away from me for my good. It didn't feel so good at the time. Now that I understand why he did it, I have a greater appreciation for him and his choice to protect me with his love.

I have experienced love so deep that not even distance and lack of communication could sever the connection. My point in sharing this is that the beauty of love is when you can take all of your love experiences, mix them together and come out of the "flames of love" a better person. Love is a refiner when you fully submit to the process of love each time. Love is not a once-and-for-all encounter. You must keep showing up and fully engaging the process each time.

My assignment in the Kingdom is to present my life for His glory. Oftentimes when sharing with women, I tell my story so that they have an example of God's grace, goodness and mercy that they can touch and talk to. My transparency is to empower, encourage and edify those that I come in contact with.

Here is an excerpt that I wrote several years ago from *Deep Waters (www.deepwaters.info)*, an online forum of which I am a moderator. It truly sums up my passion for people and presents some of the pain I have survived that has fueled my purpose. It may be hard for some to read, but it is necessary.

My ten-year-old daughter is the absolute joy of my life. She is a precious gift from God and I thank Him every day for entrusting me with her. At the same time, I can't help but think how different my life would be if the other three—yes, three—children I conceived had been born and a part of my world. It makes me sad, even as I write this, to imagine "what could have been" if I were responsible for three daughters and one son at this time in my life.

My first pregnancy ended in a miscarriage. I remember that period in my life like it was yesterday. I was a junior in college, on a full athletic scholarship, a member of the gospel choir, and my sorority was in the midst of pledging a line. I was so excited about being pregnant. I was so excited that I was fearless and ready to defend my decision to have a baby in spite of what it would cost me. I was willing to walk away from my scholarship and from people's opinions, even the people who were the most disappointed in me. The baby's father wanted me to have an abortion, but I adamantly refused, telling him that he could leave and never come back. The baby and I would be fine, even if I had to do it alone. Eventually, he came around and agreed that since I was moving forward, he would be a part of our lives. I was quite happy that my own family was forming.

I remember the night I went into premature labor at twelve weeks. It was 1986; I was in the emergency room alone because the baby's father was at work. I was in the worst pain I had ever felt—I was in labor and I was in the midst of losing a baby girl I wanted so badly. That night I made a conscious, sincere commitment to the Lord. In the midst of trauma, my relationship with God truly began. That night, God let me know that He was with me, even when the baby's father wasn't. Needless to say, the relationship with the baby's father gradually dissolved because now there wasn't a child to share. The pain of the miscarriage was more than either of us were equipped to handle at that time.

Years later, after the birth of my daughter, I got pregnant by someone whom I loved and still love deeply, but the relationship was a secret. It's ironic how before accepting Christ I was fearless, courageous and willing to go through the fire to have my baby. But this time it was different. I was married, scared, alone, fearful and bound by thoughts of shame, humiliation, rejection, intimidation, abandonment and other people's opinions.

What would the church think? What would I tell my pastor and his wife? What would my family think about the "golden child"? The baby's father was caught in the same web of questions. He persuaded me that we both had "too much to lose" if I had the baby, so I had an abortion. I aborted our son, another baby I wanted badly. The baby's father paid for the abortion and that was the extent of his involvement in the pregnancy. As far as I'm concerned, I went through that experience alone too. Once again, God let me know that He was with me, even if the baby's father wasn't.

At first, I felt relief. Then, a couple weeks later, the thoughts of regret, anger, resentment, hurt and loss began to overwhelm me periodically. What had I done? Why did I do it? I had an abortion so *everybody else* would be okay. What about me? There I was "in Christ," where I should have been the most secure, feeling insecure and fragile. I wondered if this was something I would have to deal with for the rest of my life.

A couple of more years passed and I was doing okay until I got pregnant *again* in yet another "secret relationship." This time, I thought about what I wanted and how happy this baby would make me. However, that did not last long. The baby's father and I were both married to other people. Too many people would be hurt. Too many lives would be affected and thrust into turmoil. I thought about taking my daughter, running away, and having the baby on my own. You know, desperate people do desperate things, right? Who was I kidding? I could not do that either. So after much thought and discussion with the baby's father, I convinced myself *again* that aborting our unborn daughter was the best thing for everybody else.

The relief only lasted a few hours this time. Later that same day, the waves of guilt and regret began to wash over me and with that same intensity, lasted for the next several months. I remember attending my grandmother's funeral during this time and completely breaking down as soon as I saw her in the casket. Yes, I was sad that Sugarball was gone, but for the first time, I felt the anguish of conceiving but not having three babies.

After that, I would only cry if no one else was around. I hid my pain from people because I was overcome with regret, resentment, anger, unforgiveness, misery and sadness. Once again, God let me know that He was there.

Eventually I cried out to God, telling Him how sorry I was for rejecting His gifts. I also told God that I needed His help because I could not live like that anymore. The guilt was secretly taking over my life. The first thing God did was "turn up" His love for me through my daughter. She was and still is my angel.

The next thing God did was allow me to hear a Christian radio broadcast. I was driving to work one morning listening to Pastor Jack Hayford minister to women who had experienced abortions. I was stunned, as I couldn't believe that God responded so quickly to my cry for help. Nevertheless, Jack Hayford's words were very soothing and comforting. He then began to encourage listeners to request his book entitled, *I'll Hold You in Heaven*. That book was the beginning of my healing. The reassurance that I will see my children again is what provoked me to go after God with all that's within me. Each time I conceived, my children became a part of me forever.

I still have moments every now and then. The difference in my life now is that I fully embrace and engage the love of God, and the security found in that love. His love made provisions for my mistakes and bad choices. His love nurtures my children in heaven until I get there to be *reunited* with them. His love forgives me and enables me to forgive myself. I can't stop the moments of regret from coming, but I don't invite them to stay around either.

The last thing I did (and maybe this will help someone), is I created a memorial for the children I conceived that didn't make it here. It's not important what the memorial is as much as it is imperative that you create one. You can plant a garden, add charms to your bracelet or necklace in your child's memory, start a project or a business. Whatever you do, don't act like your child never happened, because it did. Honor your child's memory in a way that is meaningful to you. There are many options. The beauty is that this time, you can choose something that brings life.

The anointing is costly. Every mess-up, mistake, mishap, and midnight hour in our lives happened for a reason. The good news is that His grace is sufficient and His mercy endures forever.

The Bible says in Hebrews 4:2, "For indeed the gospel was preached to us as well as to them; but the word which they heard did not profit them, not being mixed with faith in those who heard it." Hebrews 4 says:

12 For the word of God is living and powerful, sharper than any two-edged sword, piercing even to the division of soul and spirit, and of joints and marrow, and is a discerner of the thoughts and intents of the heart.

13 And there is no creature hidden from His sight, but all things are naked and open to the eyes of Him to whom we must give an account.

14 Seeing then that we have a great High Priest who has passed through the heavens, Jesus the Son of God, let us hold fast to our confession.

15 For we do not have a High Priest who cannot sympathize with our weaknesses, but was in all points tempted as we are, yet, without sin.

16 Let us therefore come boldly to the throne of grace, that we may obtain mercy and find grace to help in time of need.

The illumination of this passage in my life — and after reading this, I hope it sparks something in you too — is that when I mix the Word of God with my faith, it begins to profit me. How? According to Hebrews 4:12, because God's word is quick, powerful and sharp and when mixed with my faith, has the ability, capacity and strength to change my life immediately. *I believed what God said, applied what God said and my life began to change.*

Conclusion

I love the books of Proverbs and Philippians in the Bible. These two books were strength and life to me during a very difficult period. Read one chapter of Proverbs a day and I promise you that your life will change.

Philippians 1:6 states: "Being confident of this very thing, that He who has begun a good work in you will complete it until the day of Jesus Christ." To me, this meant that God would not bring me to a certain point and then leave me. He was and is going to finish everything He started in my life.

This same chapter continues from verse 9 with,

And this I pray, that your love may abound still more and more in knowledge and all discernment.

10 That you may approve the things that are excellent, that you may be sincere and without offense till the day of Christ.
11 Being filled with the fruit of righteousness which are by Christ Jesus, to the glory and praise of God.
12 But I want you to know, brethren, that the things

which happened to me have actually turned out for the furtherance of the gospel.

13 So that it has become evident to the whole palace guard, and to all the rest, that my chains are in Christ.

14 And most of the brethren in the Lord, having become confident by my chains, are much more bold to speak the word without fear.

15 Some indeed preach Christ even from envy and strife, and some also from good will:

16 The former preach Christ from selfish ambition, not sincerely, supposing to add affliction to my chains;

17 But the latter out of love, knowing that I am appointed for the defense of the gospel of Jesus Christ.

In Philippians, Paul continues with,

2 Therefore if there be any consolation in Christ, if any comfort of love, if any fellowship of the Spirit, if any affection and mercy,

3 fulfill my joy by being like-minded, having the same love, being of one accord, of one mind.

4 Let nothing be done through selfish ambition or conceit, but in lowliness of mind let each esteem others better than himself.

5 Let each of you look out not only for his own interests, but also for the interests of others.

6 Let this mind be in you which was also in Christ Jesus.

Paul continues to encourage us all in Philippians 3:

10 That I may know Him and the power of His res-
    urrection, and the fellowship of His sufferings,
    being conformed to His death,
11 if by any means, I may attain to the resurrection
    from the dead.
12 Not that I have already attained, or am already
    perfected, but I press on, that I may lay hold of
    that for which Christ Jesus has also laid hold for
    me.
13 Brethren, I do not count myself to have appre-
    hended; but one thing I do, forgetting those
    things which are behind and reaching forward to
    those things which are ahead.
14 I press toward the goal of the upward call of God
    in Christ Jesus.

Those who have encountered real love and are now
loving people give up their internal power struggle. Those
who are powerful and relationally disconnected give up
their capacity to love. The peculiar thing is that you can
be a powerful and loving person once you understand
that the source of your power is God (love).

Real love produces maturity. Maturity means I can own
all of who I am as a woman (including my desire, my femininity and my dreams). Through my relationship with
Jesus Christ, this ownership gives me freedom.

Many of us need to redefine freedom. Freedom outside
of "freedom in Christ" is not freedom at all but another
form of bondage. Freedom without accountability is a

breeding ground for abuse and misuse. We have become enslaved to the world's definitions of independence, integration and intelligence. Consequently, many of us end up experiencing the counterfeit instead of the real thing.

The Bible says in 1 John 4:18 "Perfect love casts out fear; for fear hath torment." The root cause of each and every form of counterfeit love is fear. Yet, we are drawn into relationships based on fear and not love. Why are we attracted to what causes us dread, anxiety and stress? Why do we push away the very thing—love—God—that can bring us peace?

There are many answers to these questions. As many answers as there are people on earth. It matters not your reason at this moment because right now you can begin again. Begin to see yourself the way God sees you. Then and only then can you love the way God loves and draw to yourself the kind of love relationships that please God.

We all want to experience in this lifetime that one, all-empowering relationship with someone that expands our capacity for God because we are so appreciative that God planted such a wonderful person in our lives.

In order to experience "heaven on earth" in our relationships, the trust and honesty of *agape* love must continue with the courage and vulnerability of passion in order to create true intimacy. In our quest to love and to be loved, we must remain open to truly knowing and truly being known which can only take place when fear no longer rules your heart.

Love is about value, vision, passion, purpose, excite-ment, endurance, enjoyment, exchange. Love is about what we bring to the table to share. Love is about achieving oneness, fulfillment and satisfaction. Love is about tenderness, strength, gentleness and power.

C. S. Lewis wrote in his book, *Mere Christianity*, something that I use when I perform weddings.

> Being in love is a good thing, but it is not the best thing. There are many things below it, but there are also things above it. You cannot make it the basis of a whole life. It is a noble feeling, but it is still a feeling. Now no feeling can be relied upon to last in its full intensity, or even to last at all. In fact, being in love usually does not last.
>
> Love is a deep unity, maintained by the will and deliberately strengthened by habit; reinforced by the grace which both partners ask and receive from God. They can retain this love, even when each would easily, if they allowed themselves, be "in love" with someone else. Being in love first moved them to promise fidelity: this quieter love enables them to keep their promise. It is on this love that the engine of marriage is run: being in love was the engine that started it.

The key to love relationships the way God intended is found in scripture in John 15:10. Jesus told his disciples, "Dwell in my love. If you heed my commands, you will dwell in my love, as I have heeded my Father's commands and dwell in His love."

Dear reader, where does your heart make its abode today? Are you resting in a place shrouded in counterfeit

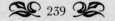

love or are you dwelling in the love of Jesus Christ? Examine your relationships right now and then love what God commands and desire what He promises.

Today is your day to go from being abused to being adored. Today is your day to go from fantasy to favor. Today is your day to go from being a sex depot to a secure and satisfied woman. Today is your day to go from co-dependency to compassion without fear. Make the move today from undefined relationships to an unending relationship with the lover of your soul — Jesus Christ.

You no longer have to over-nurture, be the other woman, be jealous, be a people-pleaser, a drama queen, a lesbian, a sugar baby or a great pretender. Come out of denial and realize that you are God's choice. Apply the word of God to your situation. Wisdom is the principal thing. However, make sure you get an understanding of what God says and how it applies to your life. *You can do this!* Proverbs 16:16 says, "How much better is it to get wisdom than gold and to get understanding rather to be chosen than silver."

Psalm 111:10 says, "The fear of the Lord is the beginning of wisdom." Right relationships increase your wisdom. Proverbs 13:20 declares, "He that walks with wise men shall be wise: but a companion of fools shall be destroyed." Is that simple enough for you? Watch the company you keep. Hang around people who are doing what you want to do or are where you want to be. You must become a passionate student and remain teachable.

Proverbs 4 says, "When Wisdom enters thy heart, and knowledge is pleasant unto thy soul, discretion shall preserve thee, understanding shall keep thee; deliver thee from the way of the evil man, from the man that speaks forward things; who leaves the paths of uprightness, to walk in the ways of darkness; Where there is no counsel, the people fall and perish: but in the multitude of counsel there is safety." When you cannot get to your pastor, your family or your friends, you can get to the Word of God.

You are the apple of God's eye. You are the prize. You are above only and not beneath. You were chosen in God before the foundation of the world and you are RIGHT NOW accepted in the beloved. You are accepted with all your stuff, your issues, your hang-ups, let-downs, your past, your present and your future. You are precious to God and your best days are ahead of you…yes, the best is yet to come.

Father in the name of Jesus, I thank you for eyes that are reading these words right now. I thank that you are the guarantee of our inheritance until the redemption of the purchased possession, to the praise of Your glory. Thank you, that right now, the eyes of our understanding are being enlightened so that we may know what is the hope of Your calling on our lives, what are the riches of the glory of Your inheritance in us. Thank you for working in us to will and to do of your good pleasure. Thank you for putting all things under our feet and making us to be head over all things — even counterfeit love. Thank you that we are complete in you right now. Thank you that there is no lack in any area of our lives. Thank you for raising us up and causing us to be seated with you in heavenly places in Christ Jesus. I thank you that from this moment, we will live with great expectation for each new day. Thank you for giving us the capacity to love as you love, both giving and receiving. Now we commit all that we are to you, because You alone are able to keep us from falling and to present us faultless before the presence of Your glory with exceeding joy; You alone are able to do exceeding abundantly above all that we can ask or think according to the power that works in us; You alone are capable of giving us peace that surpasses all understanding, helping us to guard our hearts and minds with all diligence. You alone are worthy of our praise and adoration. We thank you God because no one can love us like you can. Amen.

Now go and live your best life full of love the way God intended!!!

Scripture

Now to Him who is able to do exceeding abundantly above all that we can ask or think according to the power that works in us.

Ephesians 3:20

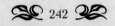

Written Affirmation

Share Your Thoughts

My life will never be the same because:

_____

_____

_____

_____

_____

_____

_____

Afterword

Dear Reader,

Thank you for sharing the next step in what has been an incredible journey thus far. *Addicted to Counterfeit Love* was a heartfelt, sometimes heart-wrenching, but always heart-healing labor of love that began with my first book, *Gems For The Journey*. It continued with my second book, *More Gems For The Journey*, pieces of which you were able to read in this book. If you haven't done so already, please find a way to read my previous works as they have been a blessing to many, many people.

It is time for the greatness of God in you to be revealed to the world. God is doing it in my life and my responsibility is to reach back and pull you into the same place of believing that God can do anything! The Bible says in Luke 22:32, "But I have prayed for you, that your faith should not fail; and when you have been converted, strengthen your brethren." Strengthened to do what, you ask? I share my journey with you so that you in turn can be empowered to laugh, to live and to love the way God intended.

My desire for you is that you put this book down and become ALL that you're supposed to be. I once told someone that I do the many things I do because I want to leave this world having emptied out all that I was supposed to give. I'm on my way to reaching that goal. Won't you join me? Thank you for being one of the lives to receive the gift of God through me: REAL LOVE!

Vikki Johnson

How to Pray

One of my favorite Christian authors, Smith Wigglesworth, said, "I never pray for more than thirty minutes and I never go longer than thirty minutes without praying." I read that over fifteen years ago and it has had an impact on my prayer life since. It made clear the scripture that instructs us to "pray without ceasing."

Many people think that they are incapable of praying effectively because they don't pray like the preacher or because they feel inadequate to approach God with their "stuff." Another spiritual insight that blessed me was the wisdom of a woman I highly respect. Her name is Dr. Cleo Townsend (www.townsendministries.org). Dr. Townsend said, "We can no longer afford to approach God as sinner to Savior or servant to Lord. We must begin engaging God as son (or daughter) to Father." That really made clear to me a very familiar prayer that we all know—the Lord's Prayer, which opens with, "Our Father, which art in heaven."

God is our Father, and consequently, we can talk to Him as such. Here are some suggestions that I compiled with the help of my dear friends at www.rebirthinternational.net who have learned the power of prayer.

- Talk to God anywhere (try to find a favorite, quiet place when possible).
- Talk to God anytime (early in the morning is a *wonderful* time).
- Use conversational tones (as if God was another person right in front of you).
- Don't do all the talking—be quiet and listen for God to respond (He does).
- Try asking for *nothing* and giving thanks for *everything* (it's already done).
- Write your prayers (writing is powerful).
- Incorporate the scriptures (His word *always* produces results).
- Personalize scriptures (insert your name into the promises found therein).
- Pray believing that God is faithful to His word (His word + your faith = *wow*).
- Prayer often leads to praise and worship (enter in and enjoy His presence).

Source Notes

Sex and the Soul of a Woman, Paula Rinehart. Zondervan, Grand Rapids, MI 49530 (2004)

Give It to Her, Sandra Mizell Chaney. Pleasant Word, Enumclaw, WA 98022 (2005)

Sex Has a Price Tag, Pam Stenzel. Zondervan, Grand Rapids, MI 49530 (2003)

Real Men Wear Boxer Shorts, Dewey Friedel. Treasure House, Shippensburg, PA (1995)

Women Who Love Too Much, Robin Norwood. Pocket Books (Simon & Schuster, Inc.) (1985)